The
MUROPHYTES

Exploring the Hidden Ecosystem:
A Comprehensive Study of Wall Flora

DEEPENDRA KUMAR ANAND

BLUEROSE PUBLISHERS
India | U.K.

Copyright © Deependra Kumar Anand 2023

All rights reserved by author. No part of this publication may be reproduced, stored in a retrieval system or transmitted in any form or by any means, electronic, mechanical, photocopying, recording or otherwise, without the prior permission of the author. Although every precaution has been taken to verify the accuracy of the information contained herein, the publisher assumes no responsibility for any errors or omissions. No liability is assumed for damages that may result from the use of information contained within.

BlueRose Publishers takes no responsibility for any damages, losses, or liabilities that may arise from the use or misuse of the information, products, or services provided in this publication.

For permissions requests or inquiries regarding this publication, please contact:

BLUEROSE PUBLISHERS
www.BlueRoseONE.com
info@bluerosepublishers.com
+91 8882 898 898
+4407342408967

ISBN: 978-93-5819-870-6

Cover Design: Muskan Sachdeva
Typesetting: Pooja Sharma

First Edition: December 2023

Dedication

I dedicate this book to our beloved Teacher, Professor Anil Kumar Dwivedi.

PEARL (Pollution and Environmental Assay
Research Laboratory)
Head, Department of Botany
DDU Gorakhpur University Gorakhpur.

Acknowledgements

I am thankful to the Almighty who showed me the path to through. It is very difficult to name all the sources of inspiration; moreover words are often too weak mode of revealing ones sentiments and feelings of indebtedness.

I am unable to find words which could encompass the sincere and deep feeling of gratitude and thankfulness that I have to my teacher, Professor **Anil kumar Dwivedi** Head, Department of Botany, DDU Gorakhpur University, Gorakhpur. His sincerity and punctuality has played a role of major catalyst in promoting the onward march of this work at every step. His invigorating encouragement and right direction at every crucial junction are also appreciable. Sir, Your advice on both, research as well as on my career has been crucial.

My gratitude are also due to **Prof. R. P. Shukla,** and **Prof. P. P. Upadhyaya,** formerly Head, Department of Botany, DDU Gorakhpur University, Gorakhpur for his endless and continuous moral support and also for providing the required departmental facilities in the work during his tenure.

I am extremely thankful to **Prof. Kamal, Professor S. C. Tripathi** and **Prof. Kalawati Shukla, Prof. (Ms.) Nisha Mishra** former Heads, Department of Botany, DDU Gorakhpur University Gorakhpur for their encouragements. I wish to express my special thanks to **Prof. S. N. Gupta, Prof. N. N. Tripathi, Prof. V. N. Panday, Prof. Malvika Srivastava and Prof. Pooja Singh,** Department of Botany, DDU Gorakhpur University, Gorakhpur for their memorable suggestions and help during the course of my research work.

I would like to thank our Grand Guru **Prof. B. D. Tripathi,** Emeritus Scientist BSR-UGC, CAS in Botany, Banaras Hindu University, Varanasi, for being the source of inspiration.

My mother **Smt. Deolata devi** and my father **Shri Akhilesh Kumar** sacrificed their comfort to fulfill of my dream and they are the source of inspiration. Ultimately I dedicate this book to my parents.

I thank to one and all my friends and well wishers whose name could not be brought here, but they contributed to bring the work in its present from directly or indirectly.

Dr. Deependra Kumar Anand

Contents

Chapter 1: Introduction 1
Chapter 2: Bibliographic Appraisal 15
Chapter 3: Material and Methods 32
Chapter 4: Results 43
Chapter 5: Bibliographic Appraisal 92

Chapter 1

Introduction

Architecture can be described as the sum of the social economic, Political and cultural developments. The places people live-in also live for years. The representation of architectural heritage has its own architectural, historical and cultural messages that have undertaken a social duty to give cultural messages to their environments and future generations. The intersection zone of technique and art is the physical and permanent sign of social, economic, and National structural culture (Yaldiz, 2010).

Plant can live in aquatic, terrestrial and organic environment. Their habitat in which the extreme condition leads to the selection of species with morphological and physiological adaptation enabling them to survive. No life can be expected on earth without vegetation but growth of plants on some unusual habitats like roofs, and wall of buildings, monuments, cenotaphs, houses, civil engineering structure, drainage pipes etc. can cause severe problems to the aesthetic and stability of structure and sometime threat to human life too (Lissi & Pacini, 1993& Singh, 2010).

Billions of currency is wasted each year just in the civil work of repair and maintenance of buildings. Still the ancient building and monuments are continuously destroyed. Sculptures, paintings, manuscripts, Tod-Patras, Bhoj-Patras, Historic building and Monuments created by our ancestors over the years are a source of inspiration for the present and future generations (Dwivedi & Anand, 2013; Singh 2012 & Singh, 2011, 2014).

Walls are man-made habitats representing a specific environment influence a range of plants species which are able to colonize such habitat (Singh, 2014). The term "Murophyte" stands for the plants growing over the human constructed structure i.e.; the building (Dwivedi & Anand, 2011).

Plants colonized on wall with specific adaptations for development and reproduction (Lisci & Pacini, 1993 a, b).

According to Varshney (1971) "building structure provides a unique habitat for the development of a specialized flora which assumes luxuriance during the monsoon period. Mural flora which developed in historical periods in which civilized man constructed buildings, the oldest wall or those most characteristically covered in vegetation, the mural plant may colonize stone work in specific areas, depending on their capacity to adopt and develop on the efficiency of their reproductive mechanism (Lisci & Pacini, 1993 a, b). The description of habitat and age of wall flora, the correlation between material of wall and distribution of wall plants the correlation of climate and seasonal pattern, the destructive effect of plants on walls and the dominance of the families and genera have attracted the attention of man (Dixits, 1983). Pants growing at the extreme base of a wall were ignored since these would probably be rooted in the ground and therefore not truly rupestral (Payne, 1978).

Urbanization imposes notable threats to global biodiversity (Li *et al.,* 2019).

In tropical region where the climate condition are quite conductive to the growth of biological agencies and variety of biological growth over the buildings and monument (Mishra *et al.,* 1995). The wall flora especially plants growing on the walls of the historical building influences a range of plants species which are able to colonize this habitat (Mustafa & Atamov, 2006).

The common growing plant on wall and roofs are identified as Algae, Fungi, Lichen, Bryophytes, Pteridophytes and Angiosperms (Shah, 1992).

The presence of various type of building with shape and constructed materials such as timber and concrete offers a unique habitat for the growth and development of plants on the building. Plants do not only refer to those trees, shrubs or even herbs that one is familiar with but inclusive of all microscopic organism that are not all that obvious (Yasin *et al.,* 2007). The wall plants are the results of spontaneous colonization unassisted by human actions (Singh, 2011).

The building and all types of walls and urban features represents a specific environment (Altay et al.,2010). The wall plants are blamed for destruction of buildings due to their ability to grow on buildings (Sitaramam et al., 2010). The floral vegetation inside the fort premise is diversified and the wall flora is one of the most prominent components amongst the vegetation (Cerejo et al., 2010). The vascular wall flora often associated with Bryophyte, Lichen, Algae, and Angiosperms bring only undesirable changes in the property of the materials by the vital activities and the wall flora exploit the concrete and help to create microenvironment (Motti & Stinca, 2010). Wall is a suitable habitat for the non competitive species (Nedelcheva & Vasileva, 2009). The walls are man-made artificial habitat, the wall plants are the result of spontaneous colonization unaested by human actions (Singh, 2013).(Dwivedi & Anand, 2014). A range of plant species able to colonize around the fragments of the fortification of wall, wall are surrounded by an open area that is colonized by natural vegetation, highly influenced by anthropogenic activity, wall represent a specific environment partially similar to rock and rock fissures (Pavlova & Tonkov, 2005; Woodell, 1979).

City walls are considered secondary habitat of urban biota and communities serving as a knowledge center of floral heterogeneity. The old and ruined city walls containing favorable growth factors like temperature, humidity, nutrients, houses unique plant assemblages and thus can be managed for evaluating floral diversity. The wall vegetation mainly depends on physical characteristics of wall material, vertices plant types and composition (Pandey, S, K. Neetesh & Singh, S. K, 2016).

Wall flora is strongly influenced by the mass effect from the surround ruderal and semi natural vegetation (Aslan & Atamov, 2006). Ediphyte or wall flora are the vascular plants growing from the moist wall crevices, fissures and cracks of the neglected and dilapidated buildings as well as civil infrastructures such as ramps of the bridge and flyovers (Hussain et al.,2011). Chasmophytes or wall flora are crevices plants growing in abounded places, cracked, footpaths, and damaged foundations of building, these are the stress tolerant vascular plants and indicates of disturbed areas (Saeed, 2012). Wall flora are generally colonized species requiring higher nutrient content, soil reaction, temperature and moisture on wall (Lanikova & Lososova, 2009). The common growing plant on wall and roofs are identified as algae, fungi, lichens, bryophytes, pteridophytes and angiosperms (Singh *et al.,* 1992). Wall flora or Murophyte are the plant growing over the human constructed structure the building (Dwivedi & Anand, 2014 a, b). Nimis (2011) defined wall flora as the host of photosynthetic organism such as Cynobacteria, Algae, Lichen, Mosses, and higher plants. Wall of Buildings and of other constructions made of bricks, stone or concrete belong to specific, polyhemerobic habitats which can be a substitute habitat for rock plants (Boratynski, 2003). Wall floras are invading the human made habitats (Valeria, 2006). Wall represent a specific type of habitat of anthropogenic origin to a great extend resembling natural faces and cliffs (Kolbek, 1996).

Wall vegetation is a special inferent as well habitats offer an extreme environment creating varied and sometimes unusual vegetation composition (Pocock, 2008).

Study Abroad

The issues of murophytes have been in the focus of research at global level also. Mural flora growing on the walls of Italian town and their distribution, colonization mode of plants growing on walls of certain Italian towns Pavia, Rome and Siena have been studied. Colonization is essentially conditioned by the adoptability of the species and efficiency of their methods of reproduction has been studied by (Lisci & Pacini *et al.,*1993). The conservation and restoration of the Italian monuments have been suggested by (Nimis, 2001). Plant species composition on the Roman wall in Silchester, Hampshire, U. K have been studied by (Pocock, 2008).

Analysis of the biodeteriogenic vascular flora of the royal Palace of Portici in Southern Italy has been done by (Motti, 2011). Phytosociological studies of chasmophytes (chasmophytes are crevies plants growing in abandoned place) of lahour city, Pakistan (Saeed *et al.,*2012) and flora and vegetation of stony walls in East Bohamia Czech Republic have been done by (Duchoslav, 2002). Flora and vegetation of wall in the town of Krosno ordrzanskie (Poland) have been done by (Boratynski, 2003). Species diversity, flora and vegetation of stony wall in south east Turkey (Sanliurfa) and the conformities and trends about the origin and variability of the wall flora in the central city part of Kystendil south western Bulgaria have also been studied by (Nedelcheva & Vasileva, 2009; Mustafa & Atamov,2006).

Preliminary report of plant communities on wall in North Korea was done by (Kolbek and Valachovic, 1996).

The unwanted plant and its effect to the buildings in hot and humid climate of Malaysia have also been studied by (Yasin *et al.,* 2007).

The flora of 650 walls in south eastern-Essex is analyzed with emphasis on the relative frequency of species on wall of different kind and comparisons are made with other surreys of wall flora has been done by (Payne, 1978). The wall floras of the Nebet Architectural reserve in the city of Plovdiv Bulgaria has been studied by (Pavlova, 2005). Ediphyte term has been used for building plant of Karachi, Pakistan by (Hussain *et al.,*2011). The vascular vegetation population of flora in building materials of historic monuments was done by the west central region of Morocco city (Baghdad *et al.,*2014). The dry stone wall plant and Lichen community on limestone dry stone wall in west Wiltshire parish of has been studied by (Presland, 2008). On the other hand numerous studied have investigated species comparison of two habitat vegetation of wall and rock habitat from various points of view (Lanikova & Lososova 2009). Dry stone wall plant and lichen community on lime stone dry stone wall in west Wiltshire parish of Winsley and compared it with that of mortared wall in the same area. The flora described therefore dry stone wall represents a distinct type of plant community specific or even of a wider range of stone- based environments (Presland, 1985, 2007, 2008). To specify the urban ecologic characteristic of Istanbul and to show their reflection to the vascular wall flora of the Anatolian side which is distinctive wall habitat (Altay *et al.,* 2010). Vegetation of walls represents a relatively poor and widely distributed phenomenon has been studied by (Kolbeck & Valachovic, 1996).

Study in India

Several workers have worked on wall flora in India.

Ecological investigations have hitherto been mainly confined either to synecological study of natural and semi natural habitats or to auto ecological study of important species. Investigation to examine the ecological of artificial habitats within urban environment does not however seem to have been as seriously. The study of the wall flora is of a special important in the maintenance and preservation of archeological monuments of which we have a great wealth in India. Secondly the ecological study of these manmade habitats will provide a better understanding at the urban environment has been studied by (Varshney, 1971).

The description of habitat and their age the correction between material of wall and distribution of wall plant the correlation of climate and seasonal pattern of wall flora the destructive effect of plants on walls and the dominance of the families and genera were given on the basis of number of species (Dixit, 1983). The floral vegetation inside the wall premise is diversified and is one of the most prominent components amongst the vegetation (Cerejo, 2010). The habitats range from hot desert to snow line and from highest altitude to deep under the sea. No life can be expected on earth without vegetation but growth of plant on some unusual habitat like roof and walls of historical buildings, monuments, cenotaphs, houses, civil engineering structure, drainage pipe etc. can cause severe problem to the aesthetic and stability of structure and some time treat to human life too has been done by (Singh, 2010). The wall plants are the result of spontaneous colonization unassisted by human action, several studied have been conducted to analyzed the floristic composition of the wall habitat in India and abroad (Singh, 2011; Rajalakhsmi, 2012; Dwivedi & Anand, 2014 a, b).

While many plants and tree in specific areas acquire cult significance very few such as *Ficus religiosa* have acquired a universal status. This hemiepiphyte *Ficus religiosa* is of dual interest since it venerated by a quarter of the present mankind (Hindu and Buddhist largely Asian) on one hand and also since these plants are blamed for destruction of buildings due to their ability to grow on buildings (Sitaramam *et al.,* 2009, 2010.)

Factor Promoting to growth and development of murophyte

The stability of monuments is largely dependent upon the nature of its constituents and a variety of factors classified as physical, chemical and biological for its decay. These factors interact amongst themselves as well as with the constituent of the structure (Mishra *et al.,* 1995). The climate of the region where the monuments is situated also has a profound effect upon the growth of murophyte and that since all monuments are post of an ecosystem which comprises a substrate as well as biotic and abiotic factors. The growth of plants on monuments or building is dependent upon several of these factors. Three most important factors which affect the growth of plants in the soil are also responsible for their growth on monuments. These factors are light, Nutrients, climate (Which included temperature, moisture and oxygen) (Caneva &Salvador, 1989). The atmospheric effect causing and promoting growth and development of plant on monument should be discussed under separate subtitle of water, humidity, wind, salts and living beings (Yaldize, 2010). The constituent of wall painting undergo deterioration, physically, chemically or biologically. Although generally factors like moisture, salt, atmospheric pollution, etc. have been held responsible for the deterioration of wall paintings in most cases, many workers believe that the growth of biological agencies like fungi is also responsible to a large extent for the decay of mural (Garg *et al.*, 1995).

Walls represent a specific environment which is partly similar to rocks and rock fissures influence a range of plant species which are able to colonize this habitat. The habitat attributes principally differentiate walls from the rocks wall consist of building materials, which are usually piled up using various binding materials of lower durability and chemical composition different from the building material. Disintegration of the binding materials is responsible for accumulation of fine-grain rubble in crevices and thus provides substrate with variable content of nutrients that generally allow early succession of vegetation (Aslan & Atamov, 2006).

As a specialized microenvironment conditioned by human being, walls are colonized only by plant species with specific adaptations for development and reproduction (Lisci & Pacini, 1993a, b). Due to the favorable environmental condition in the basal zone of the wall (where humidity and nutrients are available there), the old walls actually serve as a seed bank of alien plants has been studied by (Rajalakshmi,2012; Khan, 2011; Kolbek & Valachovic, 1996; Hussain *et al.*,2011; Saeed, 2012). Walls are generally colonized by species requiring higher nutrient content, soil reaction, temperature and moisture (Lanikova & Lososova, 2009 and Singh, 2011).

Studied on wall of building and of other construction made of bricks stone or concrete belong to specific, polyhemerobic habitats, which can be a substrate habitat for rock plants. They are common but rarely colonized because of their vertical and even surface characterized by unfavorable water, temperature regimes and recurrent construction of the walls has been studied by (Boratynski *et al.*, 2013; Sharma & Lawjewar, 2010). Various types of building with different shapes and construction material such as timber and concrete offer a unique habitat for the growth and development of plant on the building. Historic building and monuments are liable to be affected by a wide variety of biological growth ranging from the roots of mature trees that from part of a designed or natural landscape to microorganism that can be found on external and internal surface of building materials has been done by (Yasin *et al.*, 2007). There are three factors of concern, the material, the environments and the organism. The environments in which any organism lives will contribute physical, chemical and biological factors which will have a bearing on the settlement, growth and development of plants. Buildings and all types of wall as urban features represent a specific environment. The colonization of plants on wall is favored by the wall age, the presence of lime mortar, exposure to rain and such aspects as south and vertically most true wall species are only found on vertical walls and as the angle of inclination decreases on ever widening range of common species colonize (Altay *et al.*, 2010).

Vegetation fitting into joints or cracks fissures has a chemical action on stones by acids that they release and also a mechanical action by the growth of roots has been studied by (Baghdad *et al.*, 2014). Flora of wall is composed of a high number of accidental species. Difference in species traits (Life strategy, life form, dispersal) and ecological requirements of plants (Light, moisture) were analyzed between vertical wall surface and wall topes has been studied by (Duchoslav, 2002).The vertical divisions of wall usually consist of three different zones (i) the base. (ii) Vertical wall surface with joints fissures and (iii) the wall top. Species compositions of basal zone consist of plant species of nearby vegetation. The second zone is vertical wall surface which is best developed on older walls. The development of plant communities on vertical wall surface mostly depends on the level of disintegration of mortar, concrete or any other type of building material while the colonization of plant species is determined by disintegration of material on wall tops have been done by (Duchoslav,2002; Singh, 2014; Brandes, 2002; Pavlova & Tonkov, 2005). The flora of wall was growing on pollarded willows and older along or river. The angle of inclination of a wall has an important effect on colonization in that the nearer to the horizontal the greater the range of plants has been studied by (Payne, 1989). Many wall flora species belonging to different families growing on building and monuments incidentally and accidentally, seeds of murophytes reach to the germination site by physical and biological agents (Singh, 2011). The agent according to the bioreceptivity of the building materials and the environment has been concerned by (Motti & Stinca, 2011). Natural growth of vegetation has consideration influence on human habits. Penetration by roots has much significance in biologically fouling a major problem in tropics, particularly in underground brick structure such as tunnels and bunkers where the roots could penetrate right through the crevices (Sitaramam *et al.,* 2009, 2010).

Factors affecting the flora of wall include aspect, construction, shading, moisture content and the type of adjacent habitats which have an important role in providing species to colonize on wall. There is a rich wall flora on walls of both kinds varying somewhat according to the reaction of the rock and the degree of shade offered (Williams, 1986). Disturbances or instability in the main foundation of the structure and growth of plant on monuments and consolidation which increase the cohesive strength improves upon the mechanical characteristic and leads to adherence of altered layers to the main structure (Bhargav, 2012). Monuments, stone and buildings is a well recognized problem in tropical regions where environmental factors such as high temperature, high relative humidity levels and heavy rainfall favor the growth and sustenance of a wide variety of living organism on some surface (Kumar & Kumar, 1999). The description of habitat and their age, the correlation between material of wall and distribution of wall, plant the correlation of climate and seasonal patterns of wall flora, the descriptive effect of plants on wall and the dominance of the families and genera were given on the basis of number of species has been studied by (Dixit, 1983). The study reveals that plant growing on building primarily inserted their roots in roof and walls, resultant crack were created at the growing place. After the plant death the root remain in crack act as substrate for microbial activity, these microbes also harms to building materials reducing the binding capacity of cement. After decaying, the spaces emptied by roots act as habitat for insects that are also harmful for building materials (Kumar & Sharma, 2014). All structures provide a unique habitat for the development of a specialized flora which assumes luxuriance during the monsoon period (Varshney, 1971). The colonization of building sandstones by biological growth is investigation in terms of their dependence on certain physical and chemical parameter including the supply of nutrients surface roughness and moisture availability has been done by (Young, 1997).

Role of the Damage of wall building

The world is full of cultural heritage of all kinds. A large number of monuments and historic buildings spread all over the world constitute one of the finest examples of mankind's rich cultural heritage. These specimens of cultural property not only instill a sense of awe amongst ourselves but are also symbols of man's cultural identity and continuity. Therefore one of the major tasks before the present day generation is to rise to challenge of preserving this vast and varied cultural heritage for posterity. The stability of a monument is largely dependent upon the name of its various constituents and a variety of factors classified as physical, chemical and biological are responsible for decay. The factor interacts amongst themselves as well as with the constituents of the structure (Mishra *et al.*, 1995). Growth of plants on some unusual habitats like roofs and walls of historical buildings, monuments, cenotaphs, houses, civil engineering structure, drainage pipe etc. can cause severe problem to the aesthetic and stability of structure and sometime threat to human life too has been studied by (Singh,2010; Dwivedi & Anand, 2012, 2013, 2014). Wall floras acquire special importance in the maintenance/destruction and preservation of archeological monuments, great wealth in India (Varsshney, 1971). The hemiepiphyte *Ficus religiosa* is of dual interest since it venerated by a quarter of the present mankind (Hindu and Buddhists largely Asian) on one hand and also since these plants are blamed destruction of building due to their ability to grow on building (Sitaramam *et al.*, 2009). Socio- anthropological association of *Ficus religiosa* with religion appear to emanate from its habitat of being perched on the vertical sheer of rock piles and ancient buildings with its stem root junction expending into thallus like evocative structure appears logical and deserves serious consideration (Sitaramam *et al.*, 2010).

The growth of plants in the joints of the structure should be attended to as the growing plant expands its size thus widening the joints consequently, developing cracks in the structure (Bhargav, 2012). Archaeological stone monuments in India are subject to damage by plant growth (Shah, 1992). Deep rooted plants can be destructive although their roots are weak at beginning of growth, they become stronger in time and cause widening of cracks. Most of these plants absorb little water from the substrate but remaining it from the air. Although wall plants are often aesthetically appealing but the local municipalities occasionally clean up the walls to prevent damage by the plants. It would be more preferable if the clean up was more selective by allowing for plant type and degree of damage (Rajalakhsmi, 2012).

Soil plays very important role in growth of plant. The wall flora plays a major role in the vegetation of the fortress have been studied by Plants on the basis of soil in which they grow are termed as lithophytes, chasmophytes, plasmophytes, halophytes and oxalophytes. Casmophytes are one of the most interesting groups of plant amongst the vegetation thriving on the fort walls (Cerejo *et al.*, 2010). Walls are generally colonized by species requiring higher nutrient content, soil reaction, temperature and moisture. The presence of a binding material enables the disintegration of the wall and supports the succession of vegetation (Lanikova & Lososova, 2009). Colonization of plants takes place when conditions for settlement are favorable, such as a long exposure time to allow weathering of the material and for the accumulation of soil particles. The factors influencing the deterioration of ancient walls include over slanting and leaning of the war as well as drastic renovation of the wall being destroyed (Pocock, 2008). Vascular plants often associated with bryophytes, Lichens, Algae, Fungi and higher plant are the biodeteriogens causing most damage such as cracks, collapse, and detachment of materials mainly due to biophysical and biochemical process. The biophysical decay is mainly due to the growth and radial thickening of the roots of plants inside the stone which result in increasing pressure on surrounding areas to the masonry. Root growth tends to occur in preexisting fissures or cracks on stone surface and in zones of least resistance e.g., Mortar between stone, thereby increasing the size of the fissures and cracks and decreasing the cohesion between stones (Motti & Stinca, 2011; Mishra *et al.*, 1995 and Ducholav, 2002). The aerial parts and especially the roots of plants damage wall structure causes aesthetic and static alteration to wall structure and can also give rise to fires which causes damage, ranging from crumbling of mortar to deterioration of stone and even total destruction of the monument. Roots can grow very large and go very deep causing physical and or chemical damage to wall structure (Lisci & Pacini,1993).

Factors affecting the flora of walls include aspect construction, shading, moisture content and the type of adjacent habitat which have an important role in providing species to colonies the wall has been done by (Williams, 1986; Payne, 1989; Singh, 1991; Presland, 1986, 2008). Disintegration of the binding material is responsible for accumulation of fine grain rubble in crevices and thus provides substrate with variable content of nutrients that generally allow early succession of vegetation have been studied by (Aslan& Atamov, 2006). Different species will give a different effect to the structure because of its physical form such as roots, trunks and leaves and also its ability to retain some amount of water or moisture within its body or at building structure (Yasin *et al.*, 2007). The growth traced causes a string and negative effects on their consistence (Nedelcheva& Vasileva, 2009). Vegetation fitting into is placed on joint or crack fissures have a chemical action on stone by acids that they release and also a mechanical action by the growth of roots inside cracks fissure has been studied by (Baghdad *et al.*, 2014). Ediphytes are the vascular plants sprouting from the wall crevices, cracks and fissures of the buildings and civil structure such as ramps of the bridges and fly-over's. They are the feature of neglected and dilapidated buildings (Hussian *et al.*, 2011; Saeed *et al.*, 2012 and Khan, 2011).

Loss estimated if any

Billions of currency is wasted each year just in the civil work of repair and maintenance of buildings, still the ancient building and monuments are continuously destroyed have been studied by (Dwivedi & Anand; 2012, 2013, 2014 a. b). This is the authoritative work on the subject of removal of plant and trees from monuments. Growth of plants and trees on monuments and historic building is a major problem in several parts of the world (Mishra *et al.*, 1990). Buildings are often able to exist and adopt together in reasonable harmony, but problem do occur in some cases like blockages in sewer pipes. Growth of plants on some unusual habitat like roofs and wall of historical buildings, monuments, cenotaphs, houses, civil engineering structure, drainage pipe etc. cancause severe problem to the aesthetic and stability of human life too (Singh *et al.*, 2011 and Sitaramam, 2009, 2010).

Archaeological stone monuments in India include cave and carvings, stupas, temples, forts and sculptures etc and are subjected to damage by plant growth, despite efforts undertaken by official archeological departments. The surface of decorative objects and works of art are all important, so cumulative deposits reduce both aesthetic and evidential value (Shah, 1992).

Managements

The plant growing on the wall of Italian town on the basis of site and distribution, the vegetation control can be performed by hand or with herbicides. Chemical herbicide is much faster and more efficient but in order to apply them, climate as well as herbicide properties (toxicity, volatility, biodegradability) must be known. Many methods can be used to control mural vegetation but often a combined programmed (manual and chemicals) is required to solved the problem (Lissi & Pacini, 1993).

Studied on the various species of *Ficus* genus growing as ruderal flora on building of southern Rajasthan for the protection and conservation of ancient heritage, the measure can be broadly categorized into two categories- Prophylactic measure and Curative measure (Singh *et al.*, 2010). Survey of wall flora in Gingee fort of Villupuram district show the abundance of flora in the temples, which might be due to favorable pH, macro and micro nutrient prevailing on the temples. To avoid such a destructive situation a wise step has been is followed. Prevention is better than cure control method of the wall flora using mechanical and chemical methods has been adopted by (Rajalakshmi & Shanti, 2012). Studies about the building maintenance system of Malaysia that has many assets needs to prevent the assets from deterioration. There are two maintenance systems that presently applied, which is preventive maintenance and corrective maintenance (Abllah N.B.C, 2010). In studied about building maintenance there are two approaches to manage the unwanted plant that grow on building which are preventive action and corrective action. It must be taken into account at the designing stage of the building selection of material, construction of the building maintenance planning until the remedial works take place (Yasin *et al.*, 2007). Remedial methods are aimed at the direct elimination and control of all biodeteriogens. At present, chemical treatments, mechanical removal, steam cleaning, and low pressure water washing are the direct means available to eliminate and control the growth of biodeteriogens have been done by (Kumar & Kumar, 1999).

The main types of damages derived from metabolic activity of organisms are related with physical, chemical and aesthetical mechanisms. The intensity of these damages are strictly correlated with type and dimension of the organism involved; kind of material and state of its conservation; environmental conditions, micro-climatic exposure; level and types of air pollutants has studied by (Tiano, 2002).

Plan of Work

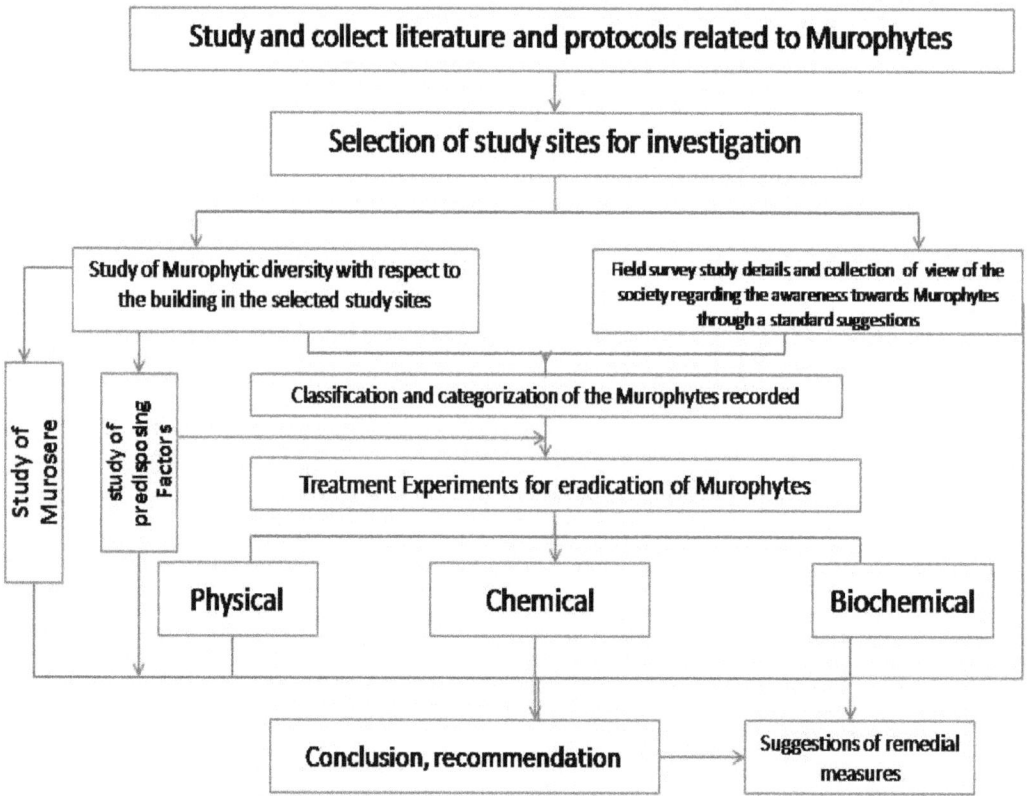

Chapter 2
Bibliographic Appraisal

Wall flora is one of the most prominent components amongst the vegetation and can be differentiated with respect to various ecological fodders. Generally colonized species on wall are requiring higher nutrient content, soil reaction, temperature and moisture. The floristic study of synanthropization show the strategy of the adaptation of the vegetation world to the new environmental conditions changed or created by the human activity. Walls are manmade habitats representing a specific environment which is partly similar to rocks and rock fissures (Woodel, 1979; Lanikova & Lososova, 2009; Nedelcheva & Vasileva, 2009; Cerejo et al., 2010).

Lisci and Pacini (1993) studied the plant growing on the wall of Italian towns on the basis of site and distribution and found that colonization of plants is essentially conditioned by the adaptability of the species and efficiency of their method of reproduction. They also (Lisci and Pacini, 1993b) studied the reproductive ecology of wall plants and found that the perennial species were more numerous than the annuals, while species adaptability and the efficiency of reproductive mechanisms are evidently the main factors ensuring the survival and dispersal of wall plants. They also observed the differences in species traits (Life strategy, life form, dispersal) and Ecological requirements of plants (light, moisture) were analyzed between vertical wall surface and wall top.

Comparison of flora and vegetation on wall of southern, western and central Europe was made by (Segal, 1969; and Brandes, 1992 a, b). The pattern of life forms record was the same as that found on walls in other parts of Europe. They also suggested that higher proportion of therophyte on wall tops contrasted with a lower proportion on vertical surface. Duchoslav (2002) studied the flora and vegetation of stony walls of east Bohemia Czech Republic and identified 207 species of vascular plants and 60 mosses. He also suggested that wall is composed of a high number of accidental species and only two species (*Poa compressa, Taraxacum sect. ruderalia*) were frequently recorded on walls.

Lanikova and Lososova (2009) studied and found that a set of 1205 phytosociological relives record on horizontal wall tops, wall vertical and rock verticals in the Czech Republic. They also compared the species, species diversity, endangered and alien species. They also observed and found that the diversity of vascular plants species was comparable in all habitat type; 242 species on wall tops, 212 species on wall verticals and 197 species on rock verticals. Duchoslav (2007) examined the flora and vegetation of stony walls in East Bohemia (Czech Republic) and found that flora of walls is composed of a high number of accidental species. Payne (1978) studied the 650 wall flora in south eastern Essex and analyzed with emphasis on the relative frequency of species on wall of different kinds. Brandes (2012) studied the 100 species of ruderal wall vegetation of Albania and found that *Parietaria judaica* is the most common specie like in other country of southern Europe. Varshney (1971) studied the wall flora in special reference to importance in the maintenance and preservation of archeological monuments, the great wealth of India. He also concluded that the ecological study of these manmade habitats will provide a better understanding of the urban environment.

Singh (2011) studied the vascular wall flora of Banaras Hindu University campus, India and found 119 vascular floras in which one species was represented by Petridophyte but no any species of Gymnosperms was observed as wall flora in the campus. Asteraceae, Poacese and Amaranthaceae were the dominant families of the wall flora and also found the majority of the non-woody wall flora appears in rainy and winter seasons of the year. Among the woody perennials *Ficus benghalensis, Ficus religiosa, Ficus glomerata* and *F. recemosa* were the most common wall flora of the Banaras Hindu University campus.

Singh (2011 b) examined the natural vascular floristic composition of Banaras Hindu University, India. In campus 329 vascular plants species were reported, of which only 5 were Pteridophytes and the remaining 324 species were

Angiosperms no any natural occurrence of Gymnosperms was reported from the University campus; on the other hand Asteraceae, Poaceae and Fabaceae were the dominant family of the flora of Banaras Hindu University. Woodell (1979) observed the artificial origin, location in the urban and rural landscape and technology of wall building and found that the wall represent a specific environment which is party similar to rock and fissures which influences a range of plant species which are to colonize this habitat. Nedelcheva & Vasileva (2009) studied the vascular plant from the old walls in Kystendil (Southwestern Bulgaria) and found that 122 taxa on wall and their neighboring area; the number of annual species were larger on the wall surface while perennial species are typical for the wall base. Aslan and Atamov (2006) analyzed the vegetation of stony wall of southeast Turkey (Sanliufa) and found that 113 species of vascular plants, four species *Hyoscyamus niger, Hordeum spotaneum, Cappris avata* and *Brassica alba* were most frequently recorded on walls. They also observed the differences in species feature (life strategy, Life form, dispersal) between vertical wall surface and wall tops. Singh (2014) studied the vascular wall flora of the Varanasi city and analyzed the flora with respect to life form, indicated the dominance of therophytes over the other life form. The dominated vascular wall flora of the exotic species like- *Lindenbergia indica, F. religiosa, F. benghalensis, F. infectoria, Pteris vittata and Tridex procumbens* were the most common flora visible on the walls of the city.

Valeria (2006) analyzed the diversity of vascular plant growing on walls of Brazilian city on the basis of transects and found twenty eight species, all of them on the downtown transect and mostly also on the neighborhood transect. Five spices were most frequent, although none were dominant and diversity indices of the six transects were not significantly different. Rajalakshmi and Shanty (2012) studied the wall flora in Gingee fort and uncared gopuras in Gingee taluk Villupuran district and found 56 species of herbs, shrubs, trees and climber. The abundance of flora in these temples might be due to favorable pH, macro and micro nutrients prevailing on temple.

Payne (1989) studied the flora of 350 walls in the chew valley. Observation was with the particular aim of assessing the relative frequency of different plant species on the various kinds of walls and studied only flowering plants and Pteridophytes.

Hussain *et al.*, (2011) examined the ediphytes or building plants of Karachi and found that ediphytic trees including woody climbers and herbs of Karachi was during the year 2008-2009 in the five district of Karachi covering 1000 ediphytic plants belonging to 17 families and 25 species most of the ediphytes belong to trees of family Moraceae (genus *Ficus*). Kolbek and Valachovic (1996) distinguished and described the plant communities of wall habitats of North Korea and gave a preliminary report for four types of vegetation. *Commelino communis, Sedetum saramentosi* and the communitiesof *comptosorus sibricus, Pilea peploides, Oxalis stricta, microlepia pilosella* and *saxifrage fortunaei, Boehameria spicata* were described. Dwivedi and Anand (2014) concluded in their study that *Ficus* is the most dominant murophyts (wall plant) and assessed that the mode of colonization of plants on the wall of historical building, houses, civil engineering structure and drainage types etc. They also found three species of *Ficus* namely *Ficus religiosa, Ficus benghalensis* and *Ficus glomerata* to be the mostly growing plant of the buildings.

Sitaramam *et al.*, (2010) conducted studied about the *Ficus religiosa* habit, habitat and religion and discussed the socio- anthropological association of *F. religiosa* with religion. They concluded to emanate from its habitat of being perched on the vertical sheer of rock piles and ancient buildings and also suggest that the plant can cause severe cracking damage to cemented brick structure within three to four year.

Boratynski *et al.*, (2003) examined the vegetation in the town of Krosno Odvzanskie (Poland) on the basis of field research in 1999 and 2000 and described that vascular flora consist of 96 species from 35 families. The predomination of apophytes plants capable of vegetation propagation was observed. Associations of *Asplenietum trichomano- rutae- murariae* and *Cymbalarietum muralis* are reported for the first time from this region of Poland. Dietmar (2002) conducted the studied on the flora of walls and ruins in eastern Crete and found that the vegetation of walls of buildings often is very poor in species, surely a result of the annual painting at Easter. In general the following rule for the species number and vegetation cover of walls.

Shah & Shah (1992) studied about the growth of plants on monuments and found that common growing plants on walls and roofs are identified as *Algae, Fungi,*

Lichens, Bryophytes, Pteridophytes and *Angiosperms*. The preservative measures and continuing treatment against vegetation growth are also described in his manuscript.

Motti & Stinca (2011) examined the ecology of vascular flora at the royal place of Portici in Southern Italy and found that 160 species on the buildings which represents approximately 35.5 % of the flora are found on the land. Altay *et al.,* (2010) conducted the studies of urban ecological characteristics of Istanbul and to their reflection to the vascular wall flora of the Anatolian side, which is a distinctive wall habitat and found a total of 101 taxa belonging to 74 genera and 33 families. It was determined that 80 species were dicotyledonous. The Families with the largest number of taxa were *Asteraceae* (18 species), *Poaceae* (8 species), *Lamiaceae Brassicaceae* (5species) *Ploygoniaceae* and *Scrophulariaceae* (4 species).

Pocock (2008) investigated the plant species composition on two thousand year old Roman wall in the village of Silchester, Hampshire, U.K. On the basis of Shannon index of diversity, to determine the diversity of various sections of the wall he found that the sections of the wall facing in north- east direction had the highest species diversity these section were also restored using lime mortar, a soft porous bonding material and the section of the wall facing in an eastward direction had the lowest species diversity.

Lanikova and Lososova (2009) examined the rock and walls on the basis of natural species secondary habitats for vegetation of natural rock surfaces and found a data set of 1205 phytosociological relives recorded on horizontal wall tops, wall verticals and rock verticals in the Czech Republic. They compared the vegetation with regard to (i) species composition (frequent species, species diversity, endangered and alien species and (ii) the ecological requirement of the respective species. The Gamma diversity of vascular plant species was comparable in all habitat type (242 species on wall tops, 212 species on wall verticals and 197 species on rock verticals. On the basis of this the wall verticals had higher beta diversity but lower alpha diversity than rock. Dwivedi and Anand (2013) examined the murophyte or the plants growing over the building with respect to morphological and physiological adaptations. They concluded that the best habitats are provided by particles of wall, by plants, its edaphic preference, and the quantity of seeds produced and the method of dispersal.

Yasin et al., (2007) studied the unwanted plant and its effect to the building in Malaysian hot humid climate on the basis of presence of various type of building with different shapes and construction material, such as timber and concrete that offers a unique habitat for the growth and development of plants on the building. Some of the plants are wild species and rest of the species that is planted around the building but spread to building structure inadvertently. They also suggested that different species give different effect to the structure because of its roots, trunks and leaves and also its ability to retain water or moisture within its body or at the building structure itself. Presland (2007) studied the vascular flora of acidic dry stone wall and summarized pre- existing information on the flora of limestone dry stone walls and proposed a description of this flora which claimed that it was unique and on the basis of this he found that bryophytes and lichens present a harder challenge.

Singh & Singh (2013) examined the wall floristic composition of city Buxar of state Bihar (India). The Angiospermic wall flora was represented by 64 genera belonging to 29 different families; Asteraceae, Poaceae and Amranthaceae were dominant families, also reported that among the woody perennials *Azadirecta indica, Ficus benghalensis* and *Ficus religiosa* were the most common wall flora of the city Buxar.

Dixit (1983) studied the wall flora of Gorakhpur, a total 168 species and 116 genera belonging to 44 different families were recorded. Correlation between their age and the material of wall and distribution of wall plant, the correlation of climate and seasonal pattern of wall flora the destructive effect of plants on walls and dominance on the basis of number of species was conducted. Cerejo et al., (2010) conducted the study over 48 texa on the wall of this magnificent fort which gives scope for detailed and scrutinized study of the chasmophytes as well as lithophytes and studied exclusively the walls and observations show that Scrophulariaceae and Moraceae are among the dominant families. Baghdad et al., (2014) studied the prospecting monuments, allowed raising an inventory of the flora populating their building materials and found that 171 adventitious species distributed in 46 families. The most represented families are Asteraceae, Poaceae, Fabaceae, Caryophyllaceae, Geraniacae, Brassicaceae and Lamiaceae.

Pavlova & Tonkov (2005) analyzed the number of plants growing spontaneously on wall and around the fragments of the fortification wall and on the Pavements are 131. The flora is analyzed with respect to the local distribution of the taxa, their chorology, life form and geoelement characteristics and observed that the hemicryptophytes and therophytes constitute the largest groups of the families distinguished by the greatest number of species, Ateraceae (14), Fabaceae(13), Poaceae(12), Bracecaceae (8), Scrophularaceae (7).

Observation on the flora of wall habitats is done by (Williams, 1986) and found that the factor affecting the flora of wall include aspect construction, shading, moisture content and the type of adjacent habitats, which have an important role in providing species to colonize the wall.

Mishra & Saini (2016) study carried out to indentify vascular plants flora growing on building of Lucknow city and found that two species of Pteridophyta were observed while rest of the Angiosperms total 36 families, most dominant species are- Amaranthaceae, Asteraceae, Moraceae, Poaceae and Fabaceae.

Wall Flora and their association with religion

Sitaramam *et al.,* (2009) studied the ecology of *Ficus religiosa* accounts for its association with religion and found that hemiphytes *Ficus religiosa* is of dual interest since it venerated by a quarter of the present mankind (Hindu and Buddhists largely Asian) on one hand also since these plants are blamed for destruction of buildings due to their ability to grow on buildings. The association with religion of the distinctive *Ficus religiosa* itself appears to be self-evident from its socio- anthropological association with rock piles, hitherto not visualized for any Hinduis and Buddhism. Sitaramam *et al.,* (2010) studied the *Ficus religiosa* on the basis of absorbing interest, habit, habitat and found that socio-anthropological association of *Ficus religiosa* with religion appears to emanate from its habitat of being perched on the vertical sheer rock piles and ancient buildings with its stem root junction expanding into thallus like evocative structure appears logical and deserves serious consideration. Reddy (2012) analyzed the *Ficus* as the survival specialists in flowering plants world. *Ficus* is hardly perennial evergreen species with variable form of leaves branches and adapted to wide range of growing condition. The genus has over 750 species distributed all over the tropical regions of the world. He also recorded that it is one of the largest genus among the flowering plants. *Ficus* species are adaptable to various light, moisture and soil condition which makes them survival specialists in the flowering plants world this plant also considered pious in Hindu as well as in Buddhism.

Biodeterioration and Damage to the building

Mishra *et al.*, (1995) studied the role of higher plants in the deterioration of historic building and monuments and reported that the growth of higher plants over the monuments and historic buildings is one of the major problems faced by conservators especially in tropical countries. These plants have been reported to cause physical as well as chemical damage. Yasin *et al.*, (2007) studied about unwanted plant and its effect to the buildings in Malaysian hot and humid climate. They found that various type of building with different shape and construction material, such as timber and concrete offers a unique habitat for the growth and development of plants on the building. The species such as fig or *Ficus* places significant forces to the structure due to its roots and has the ability to penetrate, the small cracks and holes on the structure and eventually damages the complete structure. Singh (2010) examined the biophysical weathering of building and monuments of southern Rajasthan and found that various species of *Ficus* growing on buildings incidentally and accidentally. These *Ficus* species are responsible for uprooting of plaster, widening of gaps of cracks and crevices and deterioration of upper surface of stone that causing considerable and visible damage to structures. Kumar & Kumar (1999) studied biodeterioration of stone in tropical environmental and found that many agents contribute to the deterioration of stone monuments, buildings and other objects of cultural value on this concentrates on the action of biodeteriogens from bacteria to algae to higher plants.

Sharma & Lanjewar (2010) studied the biodeterioration of ancient monument Devarbija of Chhattisgarh and found that stone surfaces are continuously exposed to physical, chemical and biological degradation. Physical, chemical and biological agents act in co-association ranging from synergistic to antagonistic for deterioration. Among these biological agents, microorganisms have critical importance in stone deterioration. They cause damage on the stone surface. This investigation focused on mycological survey of the Sita devi temple of Devarbija durg, Chhattisgarh were 15 fungus flora were isolated. Aspergillus, Penicillium, Curvularia, Cladosoprium, Fusarium, Mucor, rizopus were dominant.

Satriani *et al.,* (2010) in their study concluded that root growth of trees close to buildings can causes directly arise of diagnostic tools to follow their time-spatial behavior and found that sensing techniques as General Penetrating Radar (GPR) and Electrical Resistivity Tomography (ERT) are of relevant interest as they allow the detection and identification of roots in a fast invasive way.

Bhargav (2012) conducted the study of chemical weathering of archaeological monuments and other conservations they suggest that the consolidation which increases the cohesive strength improve upon the mechanical characteristics and leads to adherence of altered layers to the main stratum. Protections which prevents the environmental parameters from damaging the stone. Sitaramam *et al.,* (2009) studied the dual interest of *Ficus religiosa* account for its association with religion on one hand and also since these plants are blamed for destruction of buildings due to their ability to grow on buildings on the other hand. Nimis (2001) conducted study of the richness and diversity of Italian artistic heritage and found that these works of art are attacked by many organisms. The open air monuments mostly host photosynthetic organism such as Cyanobacteria, Algae, Lichen, Mosses and higher plants, were as those stored indoors are attacked by heterotropic organism, such as bacteria fungi and Insects. Caneva & Rocardi (1991) studied the harmful flora of Roman monuments and found that ancient brick structures are typical examples. As soon as roots find their way between bricks the resulting mechanical effects can be devastating.

A critical analysis for the role of trees in damage to low raise buildings in United Kingdom has been done by (Lawson & Callaghan, 1995). Nair *et al.,* (2008) studied the type and cause of stone biodeterioration in hot and humid climate. Preventive and remedial methods selection of chemical treatments, status of current research and areas for further investigation came up from this research. Dwivedi and Anand (2014) pointed *Ficus* as the most dominant murophyte and analyzed that three species of *Ficus* namely *Ficus religiosa, Ficus benghalensis* and *Ficus glomerata* are the mostly growing plant of the buildings and these are mostly responsible for destroying the plasters, widening of gap or cracks and crevices and deterioration of upper surface of building and causing considerable and visible damage to the buildings. Kumar & Sharma (2014) conducted the studies to identify vascular flora growing on buildings. They studied their impact and suggested that naturally growing plants on buildings are the slow poison for building life. Sert *et al.,* (2007) indicated the plants as biodeteriorating agents for historical monuments and suggest that many plant species are found on archaeological stone to which they designated as biodeteioration agent.

Winkler (1975) studied the stone decay by plants and animals and suggested that the stability of a monuments is largely dependent upon the nature of their constituents farther variety of factors such as physical, chemical and biological are responsible for its decay. Honey born (1990) studied the weathering and decay properties of masonry and found that *Parthenocissus quinguefolia* and *Vitis* species hold the walls without the use of deeply penetrating adventitious roots are probably they are not harmful to the building structures. Ashurst & Ashurst (1988) studied that the plants are responsible for damage to historic buildings either directly or indirectly and found that the presence of plant growths over the surface may result in persistent dampness in the walls or disturb the footings, plinths eaves courses etc. many a time these may create obstructions for the regular maintenance of structures.

Almeida *et al.,* (1994) conducted the study of weathering ability of higher plants in the case of *Ailanthus altissima* and found that deterioration can be done by chemical and mechanical process. Acidity of roots exudation of organic acids decomposes the calcium bicarbonate which is main component of limestone which is used as building material. Through the growth pressure of the roots near the monuments exerts mechanical force for destruction of building.

Cerejo *et al.,* (2010) studied the chasmophytic flora of Bassein fort; Maharashtra India Scrophulariaceae and Moraceae were among the few dominant family which was responsible for crevices to give enough space for vegetation growth. Yadav (2009) conducted studies about eradication of plants and trees from historic buildings and monuments and discussed methods for the removal of plants from the historic buildings and monuments, physical method and chemical method.

Lisci & Pacini (1993) studied the damage to stonework by mural vegetation and suggested that the aerial plants and especially the roots of plants damage the wall structure. The aerial plants cause aesthetic and static alteration to wall structure and can also give rise to fires which cause damage, ranging from crumbling of mortar to deterioration of stone and even total destruction of monuments root can grow very large and go very deep causing physical and or chemical damage. Root secretions contain structures which attack building materials; mechanical stress due to root expansion produces cracking and scaling.

Tiano (2002) studied the biodegradation of cultural Heritage, decay mechanisms and Control methods and they found that biotransformation process has a worldwide diffusion and attains highest levels in warm-humid climates, where the environmental conditions are extremely favorable to the growth of most organisms.

Diversity

Singh *et al.,* (2011) studied the diversity of woody and non woody species of Budaun district, Uttar Pradesh. A wide ranging field assessment was carried out with aim to observe the diversity of plant species including tree, shrub and herb together with woody and non woody species. In total 58 species were recorded covering 32 families they were 19 shrub families whereas 3 from herb and 2 from grass families. The total number of species, genera and families were highest observed for trees followed by shrubs herbs and grass species. Moraceae and Caesalpinaceae were found to be the most dominant family in tree species, Solonaceae in shrub species, Poaceae in grass species where as in the case of herb species, Mimosaceae, Cannabinaceae and Amaranthaceae were found to be the leading families.

Singh & Kumar (2013) conducted the study of plant diversity of Jind district, Haryana, total of 282 plant species belonging to the 76 families have been recorded. They also concluded that the ecological balance is being distributed due to quick rise in the human population and their increased demanded for more utilization of natural resources. Therefore the proper knowledge of plants diversity could play important role in planning for conservation and sustain able use of available resources. Aslan & Atamov (2006) examined the wall flora, especially plants growing on walls of the historical buildings. The study was undertaken with the aim to determine the taxa growing on the walls. In total 113 species of vascular plants were recorded and is composed of high number of accidental species. Only four species *Hyoscyamus niger, hordeum spontaneum, Capparisovate* and *Brassica alba* were frequently recorded on the wall.

Reis *et al.,* (2006) reported that the city walls are very specialized structures. They reported that the wall vascular flora of Brazilian city comprises the diversity found in its downtown and neighborhoods; 28 species were identified, all of them on the downtown transect and mostly on the neighborhood transects. Fine species were the most frequent although none were dominant. Rajalakshmi (2012) studied the plant diversity of fort wall and temple tower. A survey has been under conducted at three different temples, Gingee fort, form Gingee Taluk, Villupuram district. A total of 56 species herbs, shrubs, tree and climbers were identified from the temple towers and Gingee fort walls. Maximum number of 56 species was recorded at Sri Ranganatha temple, Kamalakanni Amman temple and Sri Pattabiraman temple. The recorded plants were belonging to families. Moraceae, Meliaceae, Rubiaceae, Cappariaceae, Areaceae, Malvaceae, Amaranthaceae, Verbinaceae, Asteraceae and Euphorbiaceae on the wall of the Gingee fort and temple tower.

Factor Promoting to growth and development of murophyte

According to (Mishra *et al.,*1995) the stability of monuments is largely dependent upon the nature of its various constituents; they classified a variety of factors as physical, chemical and biological for its decay. These factors interact amongst themselves as well as with the constituent of the structure.

Caneva & Salvador (1989) studied the climate of the region where the monuments is situated; also has a profound effect upon the growth of murophyte and they suggest that since all monuments are post of an ecosystem which comprises a substrate as well as biotic and abiotic factors. The growth of plants on monuments or building is dependent upon several of these factors; as such the three most important factors which affect the growth of plants, in the soil are also responsible for their growth on monuments. These factors are light, Nutrients, climate, which included temperature, moisture and oxygen.

Yaldize (2010) analyzed the atmospheric effect causing and promoting growth and development of plant on monument. They suggested that the issue should be discussed under separate subtitle of water, humidity, wind, salts and living beings. Garg et al., (1995) conducted studies on the role of fungi in the deterioration of wall painting and found that the constituent of wall painting undergo deterioration, Physically, chemically as well as biologically. Although generally the factors like moisture, salt, atmospheric pollution, etc. have been held responsible for the deterioration of wall paintings in most cases. Many workers believe that the growth of biological agencies like fungi is also responsible for the large extent of the decay of mural flora.

Aslan & Atamov (2006) studied that the walls represent a specific environment which is partly similar to rocks and rock fissures, which influence a range of plant species to colonize this habitat. The habitat attributes differentiate concrete walls from the rocks wall, consisting of building materials, which are usually piled up using various binding materials of lower durability and chemical composition of different from the building material. Disintegration of the binding materials is responsible for accumulation of fine-grain rubble in crevices and thus provides substrate with variable content of nutrients that generally allow early succession of vegetation. Lisci & Pacini (1993a, b) studied a specialized microenvironment conditioned by human being; walls are colonized only by plant species with specific adaptations for development and reproduction. Due to the favorable environmental condition in the basal zone of the wall, where humidity and nutrients are available, the old walls actually serve as a seed bank of alien plants (Rajalakshmi, 2012; Khan, 2011; Kolbek & Valachovic 1996; Hussain, et al.,2011 and Saeed, 2012.) The northern exposure of the walls leads to more affluent flora and vegetation (Brandes, 1996; Darlington, 1981; Payne, 1978; Pocock, 2008; Nedelcheva and Vasileva, 2009). According to (Lanikova & Lososova, 2009; and Singh, 2011) wall are generally colonized by species requiring higher nutrient content, soil reaction, temperature and moisture. Boratynski et al., (2013) and Sharma & Lawjewar (2010) studied the wall of building and of other construction made of bricks, stone or concrete belonging to specific, polyhemerobic habitats, which can be a substrate habitat for rock plants.

They are common but rarely colonized because of their vertical and even surface characterized by unfavorable water and temperature regimes and recurrent construction of the walls. Yasin *et al.,* 2007) studied the presences of various types of building and found that with different shapes and construction material such as timber and concrete offer a unique habitat for the growth and development of plant on the building and monuments are liable to be affected by a wide variety of biological growth ranging from the roots of mature trees to that from part of a designed or natural landscape to microorganism that can be found on external and internal surface of building materials. There are three factors of concern, the material, the environments and the organism. The environments in which any organism lives will contribute physical, chemical and biological factors which will have a bearing on the settlement, growth and development of plants.

Altay *et al.,* (2010) concluded that buildings and all types of wall represent a specific environment. The colonization of plants on walls is favored by the age of wall, the presence of lime mortar, exposure to rain. Such aspects as south and vertically most true wall species are only found on vertical walls and as the angle of inclination decreases on ever widening range of common species colonize. Baghdad *et al.,* (2014) vegetation fitting into joints or cracks fissures have a chemical action on stones by acids that they release and also a mechanical action by the growth of roots inside cracks fissures. Duchoslav (2002) flora of walls is composed of a high number of accidental species. Difference in species traits, Life strategy, life form, dispersal and ecological requirements of plants (Light, moisture) were analyzed between vertical wall surface and wall tops. The vertical divisions of wall usually consist of three different zones (i) the base. (ii) Vertical wall surface with joints fissures and (iii) the wall top. Species compositions of basal zone consist of plant species of nearby vegetation. The second zone is vertical wall surface which is best developed on older walls.

The development of plant communities on vertical wall surface mostly depends on the level of disintegration of mortar, concrete or any other type of building material, while the colonization of plant species is determined by disintegration of material on wall tops (Duchoslav, 2002; Singh, 2014; Brandes, 2002; and Pavlova & Tonkov, 2005). Payne (1989) studied the flora of walls growing on pollarded willows. A somewhat similar habitat, the angle of inclination of a wall has an important effect on colonization in that nearer to the horizontal greater than the range of plants. Many wall flora species belonging to different families growing on building, monuments incidentally and accidentally seeds of murophytes reach to the germination site by physical and biological agents (Singh, 2011).

Motti & Stinca (2011) studied the bioreceptivity of the building materials in and the environment concerned. Sitaramam *et al.,* (2009, 2010) concluded that natural growth of vegetation has consideration influence on human habits. They also added that penetration by roots has much significance in biologically fouling a major problem in tropics, particularly in underground brick structure such as tunnels and bunkers where the roots could penetrate right through the crevices.

Williams (1986) was of the opinion that factors affecting the flora of wall include aspect, construction, shading, moisture content and the type of adjacent habitats which have an important role in providing species to colonize on the wall. They formed rich wall flora on walls of both kinds, varying, according to the reaction of the rock and the degree of shade offered. Bhargav (2012) concluded that disturbances or instability is the main foundation of the structure and growth of plant on monuments and consolidation which increases the cohesive strength, improves the mechanical characteristic and leads to adherence of altered layers to the main structure. Kumar & kumar (1999) & Sedlbauer (2002) documented that monuments, stone and buildings have well recognized, problem in tropical regions, where environmental factors such as high temperature, high relative humidity and heavy rainfall favor the growth and sustenance of a wide variety of living organism on surface. Dixit (1983) studied the description of habitat and their age; the correlation between material of wall and distribution of wall plant; the correlation of climate and seasonal patterns of wall flora; the descriptive effect of plants on wall and the dominance of the families and genera were given on the basis of number of species.

Kumar &Sharma (2014) reveals that plant growing on building primarily inserted their root in roof and wall, resultant crack were created at the growing place. After death of the plant the root remains in crack and acts as substrate for microbial activity, these microbes also harms to building materials by reducing the binding capacity of cement. After decaying, the spaces emptied by roots act as habitat for insects that are also harmful for building materials. According to (Varshney, 1971) all structures provide a unique habitat for the development of a specialized flora, which assumes luxuriance during the monsoon period. Young (1997) the colonization of building sandstones by biological growth is investigation in terms of their dependence on certain physical and chemical parameter including the supply of nutrients, surface roughness and the moisture availability.

Management

Lisci & Pacini (1993) studied the distribution of the plant growing on the wall of Italian town site and they concluded that vegetation control can be performed by hand or with herbicides. In the first case manual or mechanical means are required to remove the entire plants in order to repair the cracks. This method is good for removing seedling but difficult in the later stage of growth. There is a real risk of damaging the wall when mechanical means are used. Sealing of exposed parts with materials preventing plant growth is another possibility of manual damage control. Chemical herbicides are much faster and more efficient but in order to apply them climate, properties of building materials and vegetation type must be known is advance. Herbicide properties (toxicity, volatility and biodegrability) must also be known. Also many methods can be used to control mural vegetation, but often a combined programme (manual and chemical methods) is required to solve the problem. Mishra *et al.,*(1995) conducted studies about the role of higher plants in the deterioration of building and suggested that the control measures for higher plants growing on monuments through physical (mechanical), chemical (herbicidal) and biological methods. Singh *et al.,* (2010) also recorded various species of *Ficus* growing as ruderal flora on buildings of southern Rajasthan and suggested the measures for protection and conservation of ancient heritage. The broadly categorized the measures into two classes- Prophylactic measures and curative measures. Rajalakshmi & Shanti (2012) conducted survey of wall flora in Gingee fort and uncared gopuras in Gingee taluk, Villupuram district in Tamilnadu (India). They concluded the abundance of flora in these temples to be due to favorable pH and the macro and micro nutrients prevailing on the temples. Abllah (2010) studied the building maintenance system of Malaysia and suggested that many assets need maintenance to prevent these from deterioration. According to him there are two maintenance systems that is presently applied, preventive maintenance and corrective maintenance. Building defects arise through inappropriate or poor design specification and construction as well as due to insufficient attention given to building maintenance. Yasin *et al.,*(2007) studied about the building maintenance, according to them there are two approaches to manage the unwanted plant that grew on building, and there are preventive action and corrective action. They suggested that it must be taken into account at designing stage of the building, selection of material, construction of the building, maintenance and planning until the remedial works take place. According to (Kumar & Kumar, 1999) remedial methods are aimed at direct elimination and control of all biodeteriogens. At present, chemical treatments, mechanical removal, steam cleaning, and low-pressure water washing are the direct means available to eliminate and control the growth of biodeteriogens. The efficacy of the treatments depends on the methods and products chosen, but new growth invariably reoccurs if environmental conditions promoting biological growth are not modified.

Chapter 3
Material and Methods

A: Field Observation and the Study Sites

The study sites were selected on the ground of their prone for the infection of the murophytes and also on the ground of their historical and administrative importance. The selected study sites indicated in figure 3.1.

1. Govt. Boys polytechnique institute, Gorakhpur.
2. Turra nala bridge, Pipraich.
3. Deoria Road Bridge, Gorakhpur.
4. Rainbasera, basantpur Gorakhpur.
5. Paidleganj, Gorakhpur.
6. Civil lines, Gorakhpur.
7. Taramandal, Gorakhpur.
8. DDU Gorakhpur university campus, Gorakhpur.
9. Railway station, Gorakhpur.
10. Piparaich road bridge, Gorakhpur.

To record the growth of the murophytes, monthly visit of the study site was conducted during July 2011 to June 2014. During the process of observation, an extensive field study was conducted; every nook and corners of the buildings of Gorakhpur city was explored in search of murophytes.

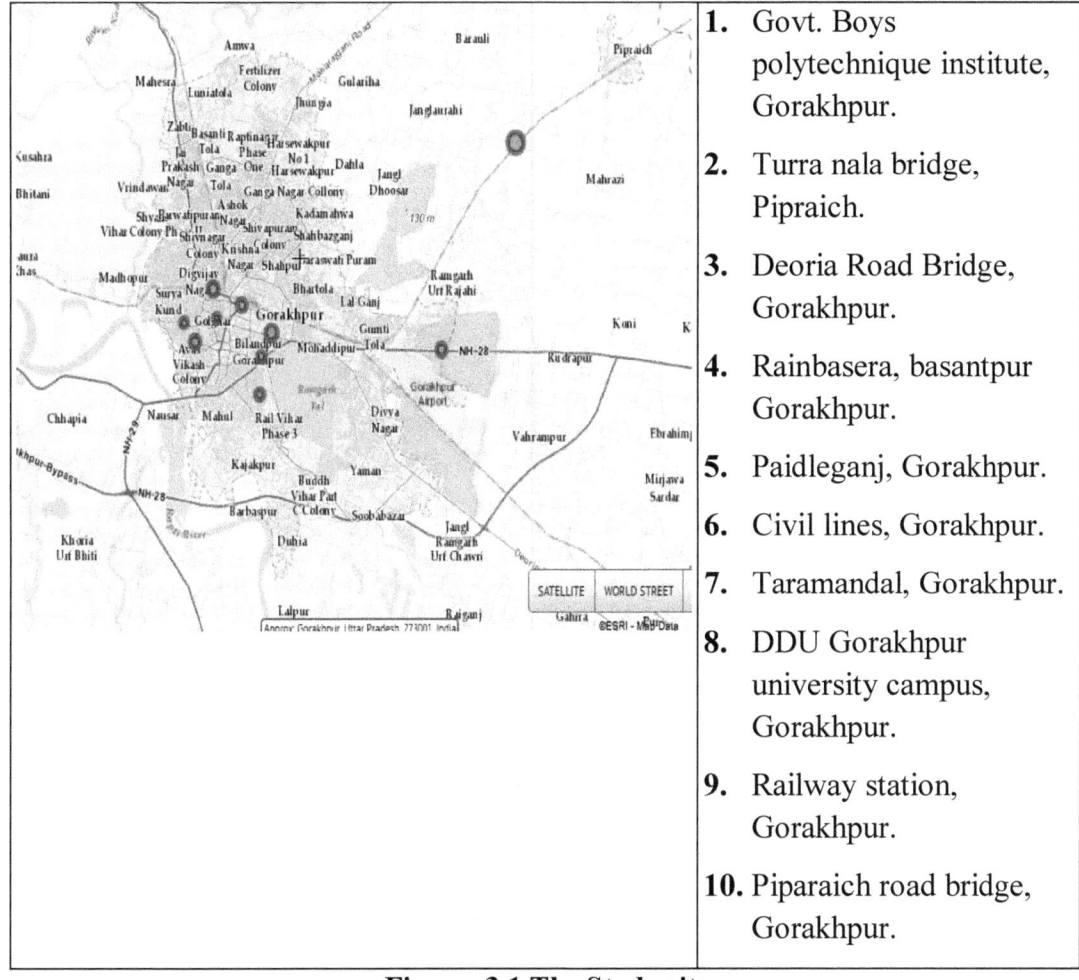

1. Govt. Boys polytechnique institute, Gorakhpur.
2. Turra nala bridge, Pipraich.
3. Deoria Road Bridge, Gorakhpur.
4. Rainbasera, basantpur Gorakhpur.
5. Paidleganj, Gorakhpur.
6. Civil lines, Gorakhpur.
7. Taramandal, Gorakhpur.
8. DDU Gorakhpur university campus, Gorakhpur.
9. Railway station, Gorakhpur.
10. Piparaich road bridge, Gorakhpur.

Figure: 3.1 The Study site

About Gorakhpur city

The plants growing over the buildings are termed as the murophytes. Billions of currency is wasted each year, just in the civil work of repair and maintenance of buildings; still the ancient buildings and monuments are continuously being destroyed. Still, no scientific and systematic study of the plants involved in damaging the buildings has been conducted. In light of the above the present study was designed. Therefore it becomes essential to study the mode of colonization of plants on the wall of historical buildings, monuments, houses, civil engineering structure and drainage pipes etc. The biophysical weathering of building as well as that of many monument or sculpture is a problem identified since antiquity. Therefore to proceed further it is essential to understand all the aspect of district Gorakhpur with special reference to the city.

Gorakhpur city lies on eastern bank of river Rapti and Rohani, a tributary of Ganga originating from Nepal (25° 5 - 27° 9 N latitude and 84° 26 E longitude) leveled topography at an elevation of 95m above sea level. The Gorakhpur Municipal Corporation, which is responsible for the provision of basic amenities and city governance, serves an area of 147 sq. km.

Geography

The city is located on the bank of river Rapti, which is interconnected through many other small rivers. There is also a big lake call "Ramgarh Tal", which has its own story of formation. It has many other small villages located around the city. In the outer skirts of the city farming is very much prevalent. It has a good rainfall every year. It is also the way to the famous tourist spot and pilgrimage site Kushinagar, where Buddha took his last breath. Many tourists come here to visit this place. Gorakhpur city is in the eastern part of the state of Uttar Pradesh in India near the border with Nepal. It is the administrative headquarter of Gorakhpur district and Gorakhpur division and of Baba Gorakhnath. Gorakhpur is a famous religious centre. The city has been the home of Buddhist, Hindu, Jain and Sikh saints and is named after the medieval saint Gorakshanath. Gorakhnath temple is still the seat of the Nath sect. It is also the birth place of the great saint Yogananda. Gorakhpur is also home to many historic Buddhist sites and the Gita Press, a publisher of Hindu religious texts.

20th century, Gorakhpur was focal points in the Indian independence movement. Today it is also a business centre, hosting the headquarters of the North Eastern railways, and an industrial area, GIDA (Gorakhpur Industrial Development Authority).

History

In ancient times the geographical area of Gorakhpur included the modern district of Santkabir Nagar, Basti, Deoria and Azamgarh. According to Vedic writing, the earliest known monarch ruling over region with his capital at Ayodhya was lksvaku, founder of solar dynasty. The solar dynasty produced a number of kings; Rama of the Ramayana is the most well-known. The entire region was an important centre and civilization, a part of the famous kingdom of Koshala, one of the sixteen Mahajanpadas (states) in 6th century BC India. Gautama Buddha, founder of Buddhism, renounced his princely clothing at the confluence of the rivers Rapti and Rohini, near Gorakhpur, before setting out on his quest of truth in 600 BC. The city is also associated with the travels of Lord Buddha's contemporary Lord Mahavira, the 24th Tirthankara of Jainism.

Mgadha's nanda dynasty in the 4th centuary BC, become part of the Maurya, Shunga, Kushana, Gupta and Harsha empires. The great emperor of India Chandragupta maurya belonged to Moriyas, a Kshatriya (warrior) clan of a little ancient republic of Pippalavana located between Rummindei (Lumbini) in the Nepali Tarai and Kasia in the Gorakhpur district of Uttar Pradesh.

In the 10th century, the Tharu king Madan Singh ruled over Gorakhpur city and the adjoining area. Gorakhpur was also birth place of King Vikas Sankrityayan.

In the 12th century, the Gorakhpur region, as much of northern India was conquered by the Muslim ruler Muhammad Ghori. The region remained under the influence of Muslim rulers, such as Qutb-ud-din Aybak and Bahadur Shah, for some centuries.

In the early 16th century, the mystic Poet and famous saint Kabir lived and worked in Maghar, a village 20 km from Gorakhpur, this place still attracts many pilgrims.

On Akbar's reorganization of the empire in the 16th century, Gorakhpur gave its name to one of the five sarkars (administrative units) in the province of Awadh.

Gorakhpur came under direct British control in 1803. It was one of major centers of the 1857 uprising, and later played a major role in the Indian Independence movement. It was also the scene of the Chauri Chaura incident of February 4, 1922, which was a turning point in the history of India's freedom struggle.

Enraged by police atrocities, a crowd of 2,000 people burnt down the Chauri-Chaura Police Station, Killing nineteen policemen. In response to this violence, Mahatma Gandhi called off the Non- Cooperation Movement, that he had launched in 1920 and fasted for 21 days, until he was satisfied that all Non-Cooperation Movement activities had ceased. It was in Gorakhpur Jail that Ram Prasad Bismil was hanged for taking active part in the fight against the British rule.

In 1934, an earthquake (8.1 on Richter scale) caused much damage to the city.

Two other important events in the district took place in 1942, shortly after the famous quit India Resolution was proclaimed on August 8. On August 9, Jawaharlal Nehru was arrested and tried in this district; he spent the next three years in prison. At Doharia kala (in Sahjanwa Tehsil) on August 23, a protest meeting was held against the British Government. Government forces opened fire unprovoked, killing nine and injuring hundreds. A Shaheed Smarak memorial stands on the spot today.

It is also the birth place of Mahapandit Rahul Sankrityayan. Late Sachindra Nath Sanyal (very few people to have undertaken Transportation for Life twice), who was the founder of Hindustan Republican Army, which later on transformed into INA (Azad Hind Fauz) was founded by him. He spent his last life as a destitute, neglected by all, in a place in the city when he was stricken by TB. The place today know as Betiahata. A large multistory residential building stands today on the spot, owned by Sahara. Also Karma Bhumi of Late Jitendra Nath Sanyal, the Revolutionarist, who spent seven years in jail, against the British, was associated in Lahore Conspiracy case; he has also written a book on Sardar Bhagat Singh was imprisoned by the British.

Economy

Gorakhpur may be regarded as one of the many Indian cities stepping foot on to the road of development. With a good geographical location and suburban to urban background, the city's economy is definitely on a rise. The city is famous for hand-woven fabric made on Hathkargha, hand operated loom and Terracota products. The city witnessed growth in industrial sector with development of GIDA at Sahjanwa road. There are branches of all nationalized banks as well as of private banks like ICICI, HDFC, AXIS and IDBI Bank in the city. DDU Gorakhpur University, BRD Medical College and MMM Engineering College are there from decades. There is also some newly mushrooming private college like Institute of Technology and Management, GIDA, Purvanchal Dental College, GIDA etc.

High water mark of the city, "Golghar", in almost the geographical center of the city includes several major shops, hotels, banks, and restaurants, as well as the Baldev Plaza and City shopping malls. Baldev Plaza is the oldest and largest shopping mall in the region. Other Malls, such as Crossroads The mall, can also be found in adjoining Baxipur area. City Mall holds a 3 screen SRS Multiplex which is an attraction for the people. Buxipur area accounts for one of the largest book markets of North Eastern Uttar Pradesh. There is also a centre for Naturopathy here, called, 'Aarogya Mandir' situated enroute to Chargawan.

Industry

Industries form the basis of progress of any space. Industries not only employ the people of the area and add to their economy, but they also utilize the resources available in that area. Though Gorakhpur is a progressive city but it lags behind in the respect of industrial progress if compared with other cities of west. The industries of Gorakhpur has been concentrated in the area particularly devoted for industries the GIDA (Gorakhpur). This area is restricted between Gorakhpur city and Sahjanwa on the Gorakhpur- Lucknow highway and 12 km away from the city of Gorakhpur. Some of the impartment industries are-

- Parle Agro
- Azam Rubber products (ARP) Ltd, GIDA, Gorakhpur
- India Glycols Limited (IGL) GIDA, Gorakhpur
- Hi- Tech Medical Products, GiDA, Gorakhpur
- Jalan Con Cast Ltd., Bargadwa

- Vinod Chemicals
- A.B.R. Petro Products Ltd., GIDA, Gorakhpur.
- Jai Laxmi solvents pvt. Ltd. Luchchipur Industeial Area, Gorakhpur
- National Ply Wood

Place of interest

In addition to above, some of the prominent places of interest are listed below. They are the prominent places of Murophytes.

- Taramandal (founded by the chief minister Late Shri Vir Bahadur Singh)
- Taramandal Guest house
- Railway station
- Railway Bus Station
- DDU Gorakhpur University
- Rail museum
- Taramandal Buddh museum
- Gorakhnath temple

Shopping Malls

- The City mall, Park Road- Golghar
- Cross Roads- The Mall, Bank road.

Main Cinema halls

- Vijay Talkies
- Jubilee Talkies
- Menka Talkies
- Indralok Talkies
- Raj cinema

- Jhankar talkies
- Chhaya Talkies
- SRS Cinema (In city mall)
- Manas Talkies
- Tarang Talkies
- United Talkies(Reserved for Bhojpuri films
- Maya Talkies (Cineplex)

Topography of Gorakhpur

The district has characteristic distinction from natural features of the western districts of the state. This difference is primarily due to the relative proximity of the northern borders, and the high peaks of the snowy range, culminating in the huge mass of Dhaulgiri, some 8230 meters above from the sea- level, are clearly insight under favorable climatic conditions as far south as Gorakhpur itself. Below the outer hills is a dry boulder-strewn tract, corresponding to the Bhabar of Kumaun and Garhwal and here the bulk of the moisture contributed by the rainfall and the small streams is absorbed by the soil, to reappear through seepage in the damp and unhealthy tract, known as the tarai. The latter comprises a belt of some 16 km. in width, running along the northern borders of Maharajganj. It is extensively cultivated in the south of the tarai, in the same districts is a stretch of forest land which extends downwards in patches as far as the center of the district. The average depth of water is about 4.5 meters. The plains form a level tract which slopes gently from west to south – east. The height above the sea level ranges from 107 meters in north- west to 93 meters in the south east. Higher elevation appears at places where the general flat surface is broken by irregular ranges of sand hills. The Most clearly defined ridge of this Nature starts near Hapur in the Maharajganj and runs in a winding courses almost to Deoria. It presumably marks the long abandoned channel of the Gandak, or some other rivers, since throughout its length it is bordered by a chain of depressions and lakes in several places pebbles and boulders have been encountered in sinking shafts for wells. In coordination to the high ridge are the low and often broad valleys of rivers know as Kachhar.

Meteorology of Gorakhpur

Meteorological data was taken into the consideration because a physicochemical property of buildings is also affected by the meteorological variables.

Climate

The Gorakhpur district has a climate, which is more equable than that of the adjoining districts is condition to some extent by the proximity of the hills in the north and the Tarai swamp. The year may broadly be divided by three seasons. July to October is wet and it is termed as rainy seasons. This is followed by winter season which ranges from November to February. During March, April, May and June the Temperature considerably is very high, this constitutes the summer seasons. The meteorological variables of Gorakhpur during the study period are given in table 3.1.

Rainfall

Rainfall is the most important meteorological factor which affects the solid waste pollution status of any city because the rainfall lowers down the concentration of pollutants of any water body. At the same time the generated solid waste undergoes putrification and degradation, as a result the aesthetic value of the area decrease and a solid platform for breeding of houseflies, mosquitoes and many different pathogenic and non- pathogenic micro- organisms is prepared. During study period heavy rainfall was recorded during January to April. Highest rainfall was recorded in the month of August, which was 66.2 mm.

Temperature

The area has two meteorological observatories at Gorakhpur and Nautanwa. The data of Gorakhpur observatories was taken as representative of the meteorological condition in the district, except that the northern region of the district have a comparatively milder summer as indicated by the records. May is the hottest with mean daily maximum temperature 40°C and the mean daily minimum 23.2°C. With the advent of the monsoon by about the middle of June there is appreciable drop in the day temperature, however the nights continue to be warm. In September there is a slight increase again in the day temperature but the night temperature decrease after September. With the withdrawal of monsoon by the beginning of October, temperature decreases progressively. The maximum temperature recorded at Gorakhpur during the study has been 39.0°C in June 2023 and the minimum 9.3°C in December 2022.

Humidity

Month	Temperature (°C) Max. Temp	Temperature (°C) Min. Temp	Humidity (%) Max. Humidity	Humidity (%) Min. Humidity	Rainfall (mm)
June	39.0	22.3	93.8	58.3	3.8
July	35.2	25.0	95.0	73.3	65.8
August	34.4	24.0	94.8	72.9	66.2
Sept	34.2	21.8	94.7	63.5	38.4
Oct	32.2	17.2	85.7	46.7	---
Nov	30.4	12.4	98.6	46.2	---
Dec	26.8	9.3	97.1	64.7	---
Jan	21.0	12.0	96.2	61.2	6
Feb	23.0	13.5	84.3	42.3	15
March	23.5	16.4	78.4	32.3	6
April	24.4	20.1	71.4	24.6	8
May	38.0	23.2	77.6	36.0	---

During the monsoon and the post monsoon seasons the relative humidity are high, ranging between 20 and 80 %. In the winter month humidity decreases and in summer the air is comparatively drier. Maximum humidity is 98.6 % in the month of November, while minimum 24.6% in April during the study.

Table 3.1: Average meteorological data of Gorakhpur (2018-2023)

B: Filed observation and questionnaire

To collect the exact information regarding awareness of murophyte among the people. Filed survey and collection of data directly from the people belong to different group from educational point of view was conducted.

120 proforma were distributed out of which only 100 responses could be collected.

To access the actual situation regarding the awareness of PROS and CONS of Murophytes among the urban population, a proforma containing the questionnaire of 40 points was developed. The printed form of this questionnaire was distributed among the people of different groups. This was done to collect and the actual first hand report. A sample of the questionnaire along with the summary of collected data is given below as annexure no 5.

C: Investigation of Diversity in Murophytes

The study was conducted during November 2011 to October 2014 for investigation of diversity in murophytes of DDU Gorakhpur University campus. A total of 56 murophytic plants species have been recorded, out of which 52 plants species belonging to 41 genera under 21 families, also only 4 species was represented by Pteridophytes belonging to 3 families. No species of Gymnosperms was observed as murophytes in the University campus.

D: The method used for the eradication of murophyte

Different methods suggested by many workers for eradication of murophytes were experimented. Better solutions were procured in the study. New combination and permutation of the studies were experimented. All methods can be broadly classified into two categories:

A. **Physical method (Mechanical method** (Mishra, 1995; Yasin, 2007; Singh, 2010;Lisci and Pacini, 1993.

B. **Chemical (herbicidal method)** (Ramchandran, 1953; Lal, 1962; Reiderer, 1981; and Singh, 1981).

Chapter 4
Results

In order to elaborate the findings clearly the result of the work has been presented under four heading:

a) **Field Survey Report**

b) **Murophyte Diversity**

c) **Murosere and Establishment of Murophyte**

d) **Experiment for Management of Murophyte**

a. Field survey and observation

FIELD REPORT

Data was collected from 100 individuals and for the ease of understanding their response is indicated in percentage. To collect the true and actual information the questionnaires was distributed among the member belonging to different group. To access the actual situation regarding the PROS and CONS of Murophytes the urban population, a proforma containing the questionnaire of 40 points was developed. The printed form of this questionnaire was distributed among the people of different group. This was done to collect and the actual first hand report. Summary prepared from the collected data is given below:

Educational Qualification of the respondents

Back Ground	Intermediate	Graduate	Post Graduate	Ph.D.	Total
Non-Sc.	20	6	08	06	100
Science	15	4	27	14	

Q: 1 – Do you have plants growth on your house?

Yes	No	May be
40	45	15

Q: 2. Do you know the requirements for the growth of plant?

Yes	No	Less knowledge	No idea	Confused
35	25	15	12	18

Q: 3. How old is your house?

< 5 Years	5-15 Years	15-25 Years	> 25 Years
45	25	15	15

Q: 4. Is the exterior of your house plastered?

Yes	No	Only frontage
70	15	15

Q:5. What types of cementing materials have been used in your house?

Cement	Brick powder & Lime	Mud	Don't know	Confused
58	12	12	08	10

Q:6. After how long duration you go for white washing?

Every Year	Alternate Year	Randomly	As and when needed
45	15	18	22

Q: 7. Do you scrap your house before white washing of your exterior?

No idea	Yes	No	As and when needed
18	35	28	19

Q: 8. After how many days do you sweep your roof?

Daily	Weakly	Monthly	As and when needed	Never
19	35	28	14	4

Q: 9. What measures do you adopt for cleaning of outer wall of your house?

Broom	Brush	Some other measure	Never do this
28	35	19	18

Q: 10. what is the condition of nearby your houses?

Touching each other	Gap between two houses	No house nearby in area	Confused
32	48	12	08

Q: 11. Have you adopted any measure to maintain the beauty of exterior of your house?

Yes Tiles	Yes regular cleaning	No	Confused
12	48	30	10

Q: 12.Do you know that which types of material has been used to protect your house?

Yes	No	No idea	Confused
28	32	28	12

Q: 13.Do you know the essential material requirement for house?

Yes	No	No idea	Confused
45	35	08	12

Q: 14.Do you have drainage system for roof of your house?

Yes	No	No idea	Confused
35	28	25	12

Q: 15. Do you treat murophyte from the religious point of you?

Yes	No	Not at all
18	58	24

Q: 16. Are you aware of the damages caused by murophyte?

Fully aware	Aware	Unaware	Totally unaware	Ignorant
24	32	12	18	14

Q: 17. Are you ready to remove the unwanted religious plant growing as murophyte?

Always ready	May be ready	Some time ready	Not at all
22	38	28	12

Q: 18. Are you aware for the murosere?

Yes	No	May be
35	45	20

Q: 19. Do you feel the regular white washing interrupt the murosere?

Yes	Certainly yes	May be	Not sure
38	28	22	12

Q: 20. Have you ever estimated the financial lost due to murophyte development?

Yes	Certainly yes	May be	Not sure
32	28	35	05

Q: 21. Do you understand the overlooked buildings are soon covered by murophyte?

Yes	May be	Not sure
35	25	40

Q: 22. Can the acceptances of growth of selected murophyte be related to religion?

Certainly yes	Yes	No	Not at all	May be
18	12	45	15	10

Q: 23. Have you ever estimated the expenditure on keeping the house murophyte free?

Yes	May be	Not sure
35	28	37

Q: 24. Are you ready to bear the expanses met in eradicating the murophyte through scientific procedure?

Always ready	Ready	No	May be ready	May be
25	18	15	32	10

Q: 25. If you are ready for eradication of murophyte what shall be in your priority?

Cheap	Expensive	Complete eradication	Temporary eradication
24	19	35	22

Q: 26. Which eradication method shall be of your interest?

Physical method	Mechanical method	Chemical method	Biochemical	Combination of two to three
38	12	08	02	40

Q: 27. Have you notice any building in which murophyte are growing freely?

Yes	No	Not sure
27	42	31

Q: 28. Do you have any suggestion or your own practical experiences in eradicating the murophytes?

Yes many (Share in separate sheet)	Yes few (Share in separate sheet)	No	Never Experimented
42	38	12	08

Q: 29. Is any building known to you which is regularly white washing but murophytes grow upon it?

Yes many	Yes few	No	No Growth recorded	No such observation
28	22	15	30	5

Q: 30. Do you thinks murophyte eradication be taken upon large scale by the Government?

Good Idea	Certainly Yes	No	Not Sure	Confused
45	12	22	12	09

Q: 31. Do you think murophyte eradication by the government as better then personal effort?

Yes	No	Confused
52	24	24

Q: 32. What do you think of murophyte eradication is?

A sciences	An Art	A Practice	Confused
28	31	25	16

Q: 33. What do you think the prominent cause of murophyte development?

Spontaneous	By Birds	Architectural fault
49	29	22

Q: 34. Which factor do you think more prominent for the murophyte development?

Wind	Water	Biological agents
26	42	32

Q: 35. Do you think the quality of building material play some role in murophyte development?

Yes	No	Confused
27	42	31

Q: 36. Collection of dust and retention of water play important role in initiation of murosere, do you know?

Yes	No	Confused
18	58	24

Q: 37. The pioneer community of Algae established the first community of murosere, are you aware of this?

Yes	No	Confused
36	28	36

Q: 38. Are you ready to use algaecide along with cement during plaster of exterior?

Yes	No	May be
24	42	34

Q: 39. Do you feel that the quality of exterior paints play some role in murophytic eradication?

Yes	No	May be
17	55	28

Q: 40. Which paints do you use for exteriors of your house?

Cheap	Moderate cost	Costly	High Expansive
12	48	26	14

To collect the exact information regarding awareness of murophyte among the people. Filed survey and collection of data directly from the people belong to different group from educational point of view was conducted.

120 proforma were distributed out of which only 100 responses could be collected.

The population lies between the education qualifications of Intermediate to Doctorate. Those among Intermediate and Post Graduate were found to be 35% each out of the total respondents. At the same time 60% of the total population was from the Science background.

45% of the houses examined were found to bear murophytes however 40% was without that. 35% of the population had the knowledge for the growth of plants.

Majority of the buildings were constructed within 5 year and 70% of the total houses had complete plastered, at the same time majority of the houses were plastered by the cement.

22% of the people go for white washing of their houses only when needed, but 45% used to whitewash their houses every year.

Majority of people were careful for the maintenance of their house and majority scrape their houses before white washing. And also they used to sweep their roofs at least once in a weak using brush. They also used to maintain beauty of the exterior of their houses.

In nearly 50% houses, gap was found between adjacent houses. This promotes the growth of murophyte because of free exposure to the exterior.

Regarding protection of exterior, most of the people were either unaware of the material use in their houses, but they knew the essentials required for the maintenance of houses. 35 % people have developed drainage system for roof but 50% people either lack it or they are not aware.

Approximately 60% of the respondents don't treat the murophytes from religious point of view. More than 50% people were aware of the damages caused by murophytes. At the same time 60% people were ready to remove the religious plants also from their houses growing as murophyte.

More than 50% respondent had the knowledge of the murosere that is, the development of murophyte takes place on after the other.

This was known to more than 50% people that regular white washing of the exteriors of the building prevent the development of murophyte and if the building are over looked then there develop dense murophyte.

The expenditure in maintaining the houses was known to more than 60% respondent, and they were ready to bear the expenses.

Expensive eradication of murophyte was preferred only by 19% people but 35% were of the view for complete eradication.

They were also willing to adopt all the possible measures for the eradication of murophyte but 50% people were willing for mechanical and physical method for eradication.

On the ground of suggestions invited, 80% of the people provided suggestion for eradication of murophyte based on their own experiences.

Nearly 60% people were of the view that large scale eradication of murophyte should be conducted by the Government.

View of majority of people is that murophyte eradication is an Art and it can be done easily without involving any science and technology because approximately 50% of the people were of the idea that the cause of murophyte development is spontaneous.

Only 22% people were of the view that murophyte development is result of Architectural fault.

42% people were of the view that quality of building material and water plays important role in murophyte development.

58% of the people were of the opinion that dust and collection of dust have no role in development of murophyte but they were wrong as per the study conducted.

42% of the people were not ready to use any herbicide along with the cement during plaster of exteriors, due to the expenditure.

And only 17% were of the opinion that exterior paint have role in murophyte eradication and also only 40% people were ready to bear the cost of the expensive paints.

On the ground of filed study, this can be conducted that majority of people are aware of the drawback of murophytes. Due to their experiences they have also developed ideas for the eradication of murophyte based on their own experiences.

Most of the people were ready to invest on the costly paint to maintain the exterior of the buildings.

In spite of all the above facts, still there were people though in minority, who are neither aware of the drawback of murophyte nor they were ready to bear expanses in murophyte eradication.

In addition majority of the people were of the opinion that murophyte eradication in mass must be taken up by the Government.

b: Diversity of Murophytes

Investigation of Diversity in Murophytes

The study was conducted during November 2011 to October 2014 for investigation of diversity in murophytes of DDU Gorakhpur University campus (Table: 4.1). A total of 56 murophytic plants species have been recorded, out of which 52 plants species belonging to 41 genera under 21 families, also only 4 species was represented by Pteridophytes belonging to 3 families. No species of Gymnosperms was observed as murophytes in the University campus (Dwivedi & Anand, 2014). The leading murophytic family of University campus were *Asteraceae* (9 species), *Poaceae* (9 species), *Cyperaceae* (4 species), *Amaranthaseae* (4 species), *Moraceae* (4 species), and *Scrophulariaceae* (2 species). The majority 19 family of Dicotyledonous and 2 monocotyledonus family were found. Seasonal analysis shows that 17 (30.35%), 18 (32.14%) and 5 (8.92%) plants species were recorded in rainy, winter and summer season respectively on the wall of university campus, at the same time 6 (10.71%) plants species were found to be common during both rainy and winter season. However 10 (17.85%) murophytic species were recorded throughout the year on the wall of University campus. Thus the study reveals that the *Asteraceae, Poaceae, Moraceae, Scrophulariaceae and Amaranthaceae* family exclusively by the most dominant families of the DDU Gorakhpur University campus.

Field observation

Botanical excursions were conducted to survey the murophytes growing on the walls of the campus of DDU Gorakhpur University (Figure: 4.1). An extensive field study was conducted from Nov 2011 to Oct 2014 to record the murophytes growing over the building of University campus. The visits were made in all the three seasons' rainy, winter and summer and five to six visits were conducted in each seasons to search of growing murophytes. During the process of investigation visit were made to every nook and corner of the building in search of murophytes. The occurrence of seasonal appearance and number of species were counted at each building plants were collected and identified with the help of local floras.

The survey of the following building are Administrative building, Art faculty, Biotechnology department, Central Library, Botany Research building, Chemistry research building, Deeksha bhawan, Law department, Geography department, Majeethia bhawan, Zoology research building, and Pant bhawan.

A total of 52 Angiospermic plant species were observed in addition to 4 species of Pteridophytes. No any species of Gymnosperms was reported from the wall of DDU Gorakhpur University campus, this finding was parallel to (Figure: 4.2 & 4.3).

The Angiosperms were represented by 41 genera and 52 species belonging to 21 families of which 19 were represented by dicotyledonous families while 2 were represented by monocotyledonous family (Table: 4.2).

Table 4.1: Murophytes of DDU Gorakhpur University Campus, Gorakhpur

Family	Plant species	Buildings of DDU Gorakhpur University, Gorakhpur												Total no of plants on buildings
		A	B	C	D	E	F	G	H	I	J	K	L	
Acanthaceae	*Peristrophe bicalyculata*												✓	01
Amaranthaceae	*Achyrenthus aspera*	✓		✓	✓	✓		✓				✓	✓	07
	Alternanthera sessilis				✓				✓		✓			03
	Amaranthus spinosus	✓	✓	✓	✓			✓	✓		✓		✓	08
	Amaranthus viridis	✓	✓							✓	✓			04
Apocynaceae	*Catheranthus roseus*	✓			✓	✓		✓					✓	05
Asclepiadaceae	*Calotropis procera*	✓	✓					✓						03

Family	Species													Total
Asteraceae	*Ageratum conyzoides*	✓					✓					✓	03
	Blumea aromatic	✓	✓	✓	✓	✓	✓	✓	✓	✓	✓	✓	12
	Eclipta alba				✓		✓						02
	Parthenium hysterophorus				✓		✓					✓	03
	Sonchus arvensis	✓	✓	✓	✓	✓	✓	✓	✓			✓	10
	Sonchus oleraceus	✓			✓			✓	✓	✓		✓	06
	Taraxacum officinale	✓			✓	✓						✓	03
	Tridex procumbens	✓		✓	✓			✓			✓	✓	06
	Vernonia strumarium	✓	✓	✓	✓	✓	✓	✓	✓	✓	✓	✓	12
Chenopodiaceae	*Chenopodium album*	✓				✓					✓		03
Cucurbitaceae	*Coccinia grandis*	✓		✓			✓				✓		04
Cyperaceae	*Cyperus compressus*		✓						✓	✓	✓	✓	05
	Cyperus difformis		✓			✓			✓		✓	✓	05
	Cyperus rotundus	✓		✓		✓			✓		✓		05
	Kyllinga triceps											✓	01
Euphorbiaceae	*Acylypha indica*	✓	✓	✓	✓	✓	✓	✓	✓	✓	✓	✓	12

		1	2	3	4	5	6	7	8	9	10	11	12	Total
	Euphorbia hirta	✓		✓		✓	✓			✓	✓	✓		07
	Phylenthus niruri	✓	✓	✓	✓	✓	✓	✓	✓	✓	✓	✓	✓	12
Lamiaceae	*Hyptis suaveolens*	✓	✓	✓	✓	✓	✓	✓	✓	✓	✓	✓	✓	12
Miliaceae	*Azadirachta indica*	✓		✓	✓				✓	✓	✓			06
Moraceae	*Ficusreligiosa*	✓	✓	✓	✓	✓	✓	✓	✓	✓	✓	✓	✓	12
	Ficus benghalensis	✓	✓	✓	✓	✓	✓	✓	✓	✓	✓	✓	✓	12
	Ficus glomarata	✓			✓	✓	✓			✓	✓	✓	✓	07
	Ficus virance		✓								✓	✓		03
Nyctaginaceae	*Boerhavia diffusa*										✓	✓		02
Oxalidaceae	*Oxalis corniculata*	✓	✓	✓				✓	✓	✓	✓	✓	✓	08
Piperaceae	*Peperomia pellucid*					✓							✓	02
Poaceae	*Cynodon dactylon*	✓	✓	✓	✓	✓	✓	✓	✓	✓	✓	✓	✓	12
	Chloris virgata	✓	✓	✓	✓	✓	✓	✓	✓	✓	✓	✓	✓	12
	Eleusine indica	✓	✓	✓	✓	✓	✓	✓	✓	✓	✓	✓	✓	12
	Dactyloctenium aegyptium	✓		✓		✓	✓		✓	✓	✓	✓	✓	08
	Digitaria sanguinalis	✓	✓				✓	✓	✓				✓	06
	Digitaria marginata	✓	✓	✓		✓		✓		✓	✓	✓	✓	08
	Echinochloa	✓		✓	✓		✓		✓	✓	✓	✓		08

Family	Species	1	2	3	4	5	6	7	8	9	10	11	12	Total
	colonum													
	Setaria glauca		✓			✓			✓					03
	Sporobolus diander	✓							✓		✓		✓	04
Primulaceae	Anagalis arvensis			✓								✓	✓	03
Rubiaceae	Oldenlandia corymbosa	✓	✓		✓	✓		✓	✓	✓	✓	✓	✓	10
	Oldenlandia dichotoma	✓	✓		✓		✓		✓	✓		✓	✓	08
	Oldenlandia diffusa	✓	✓	✓	✓	✓	✓	✓	✓	✓	✓	✓	✓	12
Scrophulariaceae	Lindenbergia indica	✓	✓			✓	✓	✓			✓	✓	✓	09
	Lindernia crustacean	✓	✓	✓			✓					✓	✓	06
	Scoparia dulcis	✓	✓	✓	✓	✓	✓	✓	✓	✓	✓	✓	✓	12
Solanaceae	Solanum nigrum	✓				✓	✓					✓	✓	05
Verbenaceae	Lantana camara		✓		✓		✓				✓			04
Pteridophytes	Dryopteris filix-mas	✓	✓	✓	✓	✓	✓	✓	✓	✓	✓	✓	✓	12
	Adiantum											✓		01
	Pteridium	✓	✓	✓	✓	✓	✓	✓	✓	✓	✓	✓	✓	12
	Pteris ansiformis	✓	✓	✓	✓	✓	✓	✓		✓	✓	✓	✓	11
	Total no of Species	43	32	29	32	28	29	31	27	29	32	39	46	

A – Administrative building, **B** – Art Faculty, **C** –Biotechnology Dept. **D** – Central Library, **E** – Botany Research building, **F** – Chemistry Research building, **G** -Deeksha bhawan, **H** – Law faculty, **I** – Geography Dept., **J** –Majithiya Bhawan, **K** – Zoology Research building, **L** – Pant Bhawan.

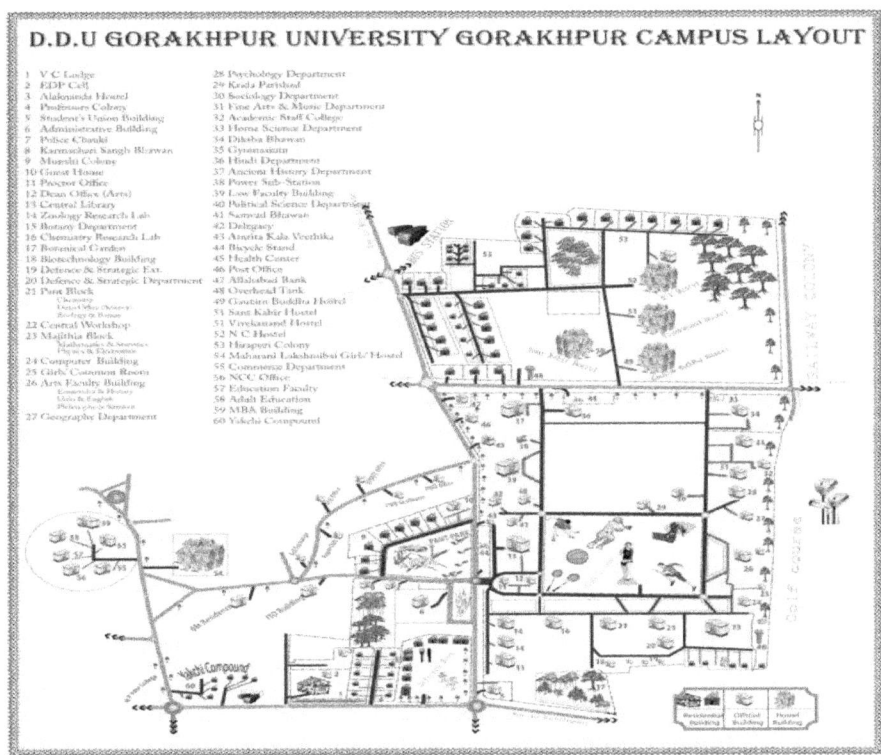

Figure 4.1: Map of DDU Gorakhpur University

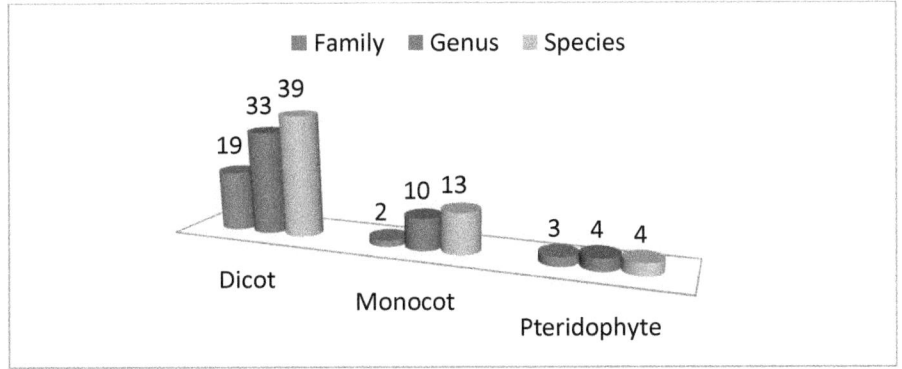

Figure 4.2: Number of murophytic family, genus and species within dicots and monocots in DDU Gorakhpur University Campus.

Table 4.2: Dominating murophytic families of angiosperm in DDU Gorakhpur University Campus. Gorakhpur.

Family	Genus	Species
Asteraceae	08	09
Poaceae	08	09
Cyperaceae	02	04
Amarathaceae	03	04
Moraceae	01	04
Scrophulariaceae	01	02

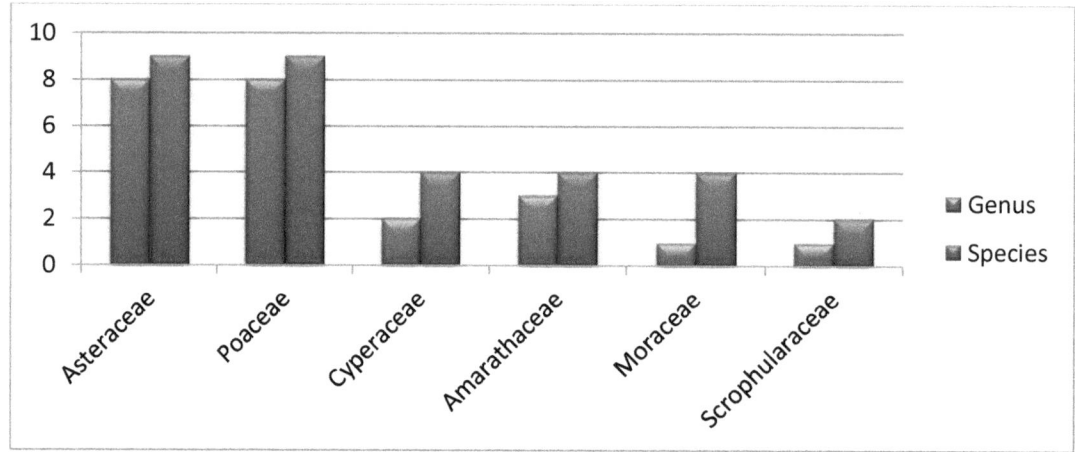

Figure 4.3: Dominating murophytic families of angiosperm in DDU Gorakhpur University Campus. Gorakhpur.

Of the total 52 Angiosperms species were recorded the maximum number of species showed (Figure: 4.3) and (Figure: 4.4) that is 9 (16.07%) belongs to Asteraceae family, 8 (14.28%) to Poaceae whereas 4 (7.14%) species were represented by Moraceae family this finding was parallel to (Table: 4.3).

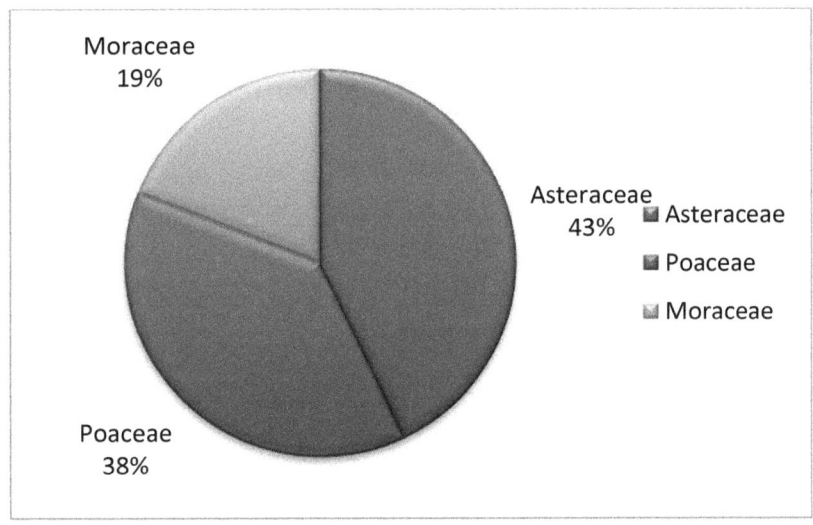

Figure 4.4: Dominating murophytic families of angiosperm in *DDU Gorakhpur University Campus*. Gorakhpur.

Thus the study reveals that *Asteraceae, Poaceae* and *Moraceae* are the dominant murophytic family of Deen Dayal Upadhayay Gorakhpur University campus.

It was observed that mostly the Asteraceae and Rubiaceae member exclusively colonize on the wall in winter season while the Poaceae and Cyperaceae member colonize in rainy season. On the other hand Amaranthaceae members generally colonize on the walls in summer season. In this study 17 (30.35%), 18 (32.14%) and 5 (8.92%) plants species were recorded in rainy, winter and summer seasons respectively. However 6 (10.71%) plant species were observed during both rainy and winter seasons and 10 (17.85%) murophytes species were recorded throughout the year on the walls.

Thus it is evident from the study that most of the murophytes colonizes the walls during rainy season and winter season.

Several of the murophyte inhibiting the walls of Gorakhpur University Campus in the present study like; *Achyrenthus aspera, Amaranthus spinosus, Amranthus viridis, Boerhavia diffusa, Euphorbia hirta, Tridex procumbens, Sonchus arvensis, Sonnchus oteraceus, oxalis corniculata, Ageratum conyzoides, Chenopodium album, Solanum nigrum, Cynodon dactylon, Ficus benghalensis, Ficus religiosa, Ficus virens, Ficus glomerata, and Dryopteris filix-mas,*

Adiantum capillus-veneris, Pteridium aquilinum, and *Pteris ansiformis* have also been observed as murophyte in other studies conducted on wall habitats.

The most commonly visible murophyte on the walls of the DDU Gorakhpur University Campus in rainy season include; *Acylypha indica, Blumea aromatic, Eclipta alba, Cyperus compressus, Cyperus difformis, Cyperus rotundus, Kyllinga triceps, Peperomia pellucid, Chloris virgata, Dactyloctenium aegyptium, Digitaria sanguinalis, Digitaria marginata, Echinochloa colonum, Lindenbergia indica,* and *Lindernia crustacean.*

The commonly occurring murophytes of the University campus in winter season is represented by *Catheranthus roseus, sonchus arvensis, Sonchus oleraceus, Taraxacum officinale, Chenopodium album, Oldenlandia corymbosa, Oldenlandia dicotoma, Oldenlandia diffusa, Solanum nigrum, Gnaphaliumindicum,* and *Ageratum conzoites.*

The common summer season murophytes of DDU Gorakhpur University Campus is represented by *Amaranthus viridis, Tridex procumbens, Eleusine indica, Scoparia dulcis, Achyranthus aspera,* and *Cynadon dactylon.* (Table: 4.3).

Calotropis procera, and *Tinospora cordifolia* are reported first time as murophyte visible on the walls of DDU University Campus.

Table 4.3: Species found in the Campus of DDU Gorakhpur University, Gorakhpur

S.No	Name of Species	Family	No. of buildings where found	Seasonal appearance
1.	*Peristrophe bicalyculata*	**Acantheceae**	1	Winter
2.	*Achyrenthus aspera*	**Amaranthaceae**	07	Whole year
3.	*Alternanthera sessilis*	"	03	Rainy & Winter
4.	*Amaranthus spinosus*	"	07	Rainy & Winter
5.	*Amaranthus viridis*	"	04	Summer
6.	*Catheranthus roseus*	**Apocynaceae**	05	Winter
7.	*Calotropis procera*	**Asclepiadaceae**	03	Whole year

8.	*Ageratum conyzoides*	**Asteraceae**	03	Summer
9.	*Blumea aromatica*	"	12	Rainy
10.	*Eclipta alba*	"	02	Rainy
11.	*Parthenium hysterophorus*	"	04	Whole year
12.	*Sonchus arvensis*	"	10	Winter
13.	*Sonchus oleraceus*	"	06	Winter
14.	*Taraxacum officinale*	"	03	Winter
15.	*Tridex procumbens*	"	06	Summer
16.	*Vernonia strumarium*	"	12	Winter
17.	*Chenopodium album*	**Chenopodiaceae**	02	Winter
18.	*Coccinia grandis*	**Cucurbitaceae**	04	Winter
19.	*Cyperus compressus*	**Cyperaceae**	05	Rainy
20.	*Cyperus difformis*	"	05	Rainy
21.	*Cyperus rotundus*	"	05	Rainy
22.	*Kyllinga triceps*	"	01	Rainy
23.	*Acylypha indica*	**Euphorbiaceae**	12	Rainy
24.	*Euphorbia hirta*	"	07	Rainy & Winter
25.	*Phylenthus niruri*	"	12	Rainy & Winter
26.	*Hyptis suaveolens*	**Lamiaceae**	12	Rainy
27.	*Azadirachta indica*	**Miliaceae**	06	Whole year
28.	*Ficusreligiosa*	**Moraceae**	12	Whole year
29.	*Ficus benghalensis*	"	12	Whole year
30.	*Ficus glomarata*	"	07	Whole year
31.	*Ficus virens*	"	03	Whole year
32.	*Boerhavia diffusa*	**Nyctaginaceae**	02	Rainy & Winter
33.	*Oxalis corniculata*	**Oxalidaceae**	08	Rainy & Winter

34.	*Peperomia pellucid*	**Piperaceae**	02	Rainy
35.	*Cynodon dactylon*	**Poaceae**	12	Whole year
36.	*Chloris virgata*	"	12	Rainy
37.	*Eleusine indica*	"	12	Summer
38.	*Dactyloctenium Aegyptium*	"	08	Rainy
39.	*Digitaria sanguinalis*	"	06	Rainy
40.	*Digitaria marginata*	"	08	Rainy
41.	*Echinochloa colonum*	"	08	Rainy
42.	*Setaria glauca*	"	03	Winter
43.	*Sporobolus diander*	"	04	Rainy
44.	*Anagalis arvensis*	**Primulaceae**	03	Winter
45.	*Oldenlandia corymbosa*	**Rubiaceae**	10	Winter
46.	*Oldenlandia dichotoma*	"	08	Winter
47.	*Oldenlandia diffusa*	"	12	Winter
48.	*Lindenbergia indica*	**Scrophulariaceae**	09	Rainy
49.	*Lindernia crustacean*	"	06	Rainy
50.	*Scoparia dulcis*	"	12	Summer
51.	*Solanum nigrum*	**Solanaceae**	05	Winter
52.	*Lantana camara*	**Verbenaceae**	04	Whole year
53.	*Dryopteris filix-mas*	**Pteridophytes**	12	Winter
54.	*Adiantum*	"	01	Winter
55	*Pteridium*	"	12	Winter
56.	*Pteris ansiformis*	"	11	Winter

Conclusion

It can be concluded from the study that murophyte on the wall of the DDU Gorakhpur University campus is dominated by Angiosperms. The most of the murophytes appears during the rainy season and winter seasons of the year. The study provides that the Asteraceae, Poaceae, Moraceae, Scrophulariaceae and Amaranthaceae families represented exclusively by the most dominant murophytes of DDU Gorakhpur University Campus.

c: Murosere and establishment of murophyte

Murophytes is a novel hybrid term, the original terms "mural" stands for wall and the term "phytes" stands for "the plants" or the flora. Therefore, the term murophytes means "the plants growing over the walls or buildings". The biophysical weathering of building as well as that of many monuments is a problem identified since antiquity. The study deal with the various species of genus *Ficus* found growing over the buildings and playing very dominant role in damaging the buildings. The three *Ficus* species, *Ficus religiosa*, *Ficus benghalensis* and *Ficus glomerata* are mostly growing over the buildings. These three *Ficus* species are mostly responsible for uprooting of plasters, widening of gap or cracks and crevices and deterioration of upper surface of building and causing considerable and visible damage of the buildings. Seeds of *Ficus* species are produced by method of dispersal or by physical and biological agents. *Ficus* has proved to be the most successful murophyte because of its tendency of adaptability in adverse situations. Extremely high growth rate of roots of *Ficus benghalensis* growing murophyte was recorded in a part of an experiment (Figure: 4.5).

Similar to different serial stages in succession in water, and sand different serial stages are found to exist in the case murophytes. Parallel to hydrosere and psammosere, murosere has its existence. Thus, the term murosere stands for different serial stages in succession and establishment of murophytes.

The initial plats are ephemerals, i.e. having very short life span. Soon they die and decompose to add organic matter in the soil deposition in various points of collection. The mineral component is contributed by the deposited dust (Figure:

4.12 & 4.13). Thus a healthy soil, rich in minerals and organic matter becomes the substratum of the second generation of plants over the buildings (Plate: 2).

Due to continuous addition of mineral and organic matters, the amount of soil accumulation shows exponential growth year after year (Figure: 4.18). On some specific sites indicated in plate 2. The amount of accumulated soil forms the base and substratum to support the growth of higher plants. Thus, the primary community is algae, followed by secondary community as bryophytes, grasses and lower angiosperms form the tertiary community and finally the higher angiosperms form the quaternary community. The point of special interest in Murosere is that one community does not replace the other; instead one community invites the other. Thus, in the final community all the communities, such as primary, secondary, tertiary as well as quaternary community show co-existence (Figure: 4.17 and Annexure 2).

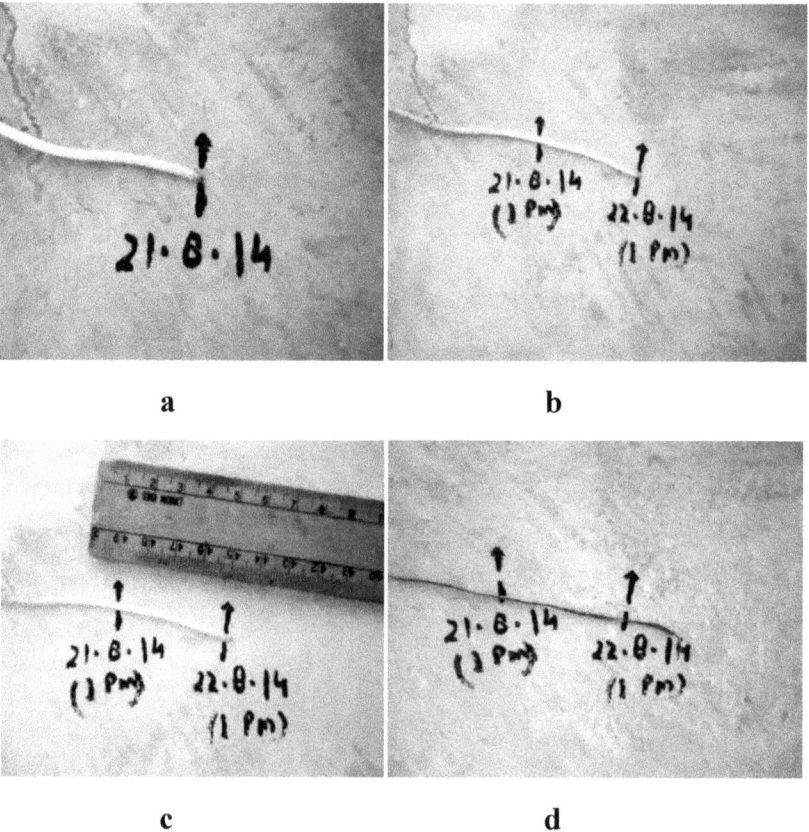

Figure 4.5: (a, b, c, and d) plates showing high growth rate of root of *Ficus benghalensis*

Architecture can be described as the sum of the social economic political and cultural developments. The places people live in also live for years. The representative of architectural heritage each has its own architectural historical and cultural message have undertaken a social duty to give cultural message to their environment and future generation. Architecture taking place at the intersection zone of technique and art is the physical and permanent sign of social and economic life cultural and national structural cultural (Mishra *et al.,* 2000).

The historical monuments sustained from past to present have worn out to various effects and disappeared in short periods due to lack of care. The deteriorations on the construction materials have occurred not only because of the year but also mostly due to the environment and the other is material of construction. The buildings are unfavorably affected from changing natural environment and climate conditions. Climate can be defined as the whole atmospheric events such as rain fall, temperature, wind, pressure and humidity that cause certain damages on the monumental buildings for years.

Plant can live in aquatic, terrestrial and organic environments. Their growth influenced by many parameters. There are habitats in which the extreme condition leads to the selection of species with morphological and physiological adaptation enabling them to survive (Figure: 4.7). Walls constitute a specialized microhabitat; since they are built by man, they are restricted to inhibited areas. Murophytes developed in historical periods in which civilized man constructed buildings .The oldest wall or those most characteristically covered in vegetation. In general it is possible to distinguish stone which is an integral part of inhibited building, stonework on the ground (part of old fortifications, roads, etc.) and isolated walls. The best habitats are provided by retaining walls; through the cracks the earth supplies moisture, particles of soil and nutrients. Hence the factors promoting the colonization of a wall by murophytes are its edaphic preferences, the quantity of seeds produced and the method of dispersal (Sitaramam *et al.,* 1974).

The following predominating factors (Figure: 4.6) are responsible for growth and developments of murophytes:

➢ Availability of water

➢ Exposure

- Light
- Substrate
- Nutrients
- Shady place
- Birds excitements
- Type of building structure

Edaphic Preferences

Specie and environment dependent:

- Volume of substrate available
- Type of substrate
- Exposure
- Moisture requirements for germination and reproduction

Dispersal Methods

In order of decreasing advantage:

- Anemochory due to lightness of seeds
- Anemochory due to special structures(pappi, wings, etc.)
- Myrmecochory
- Zoochory
- Other dispersal mechanism

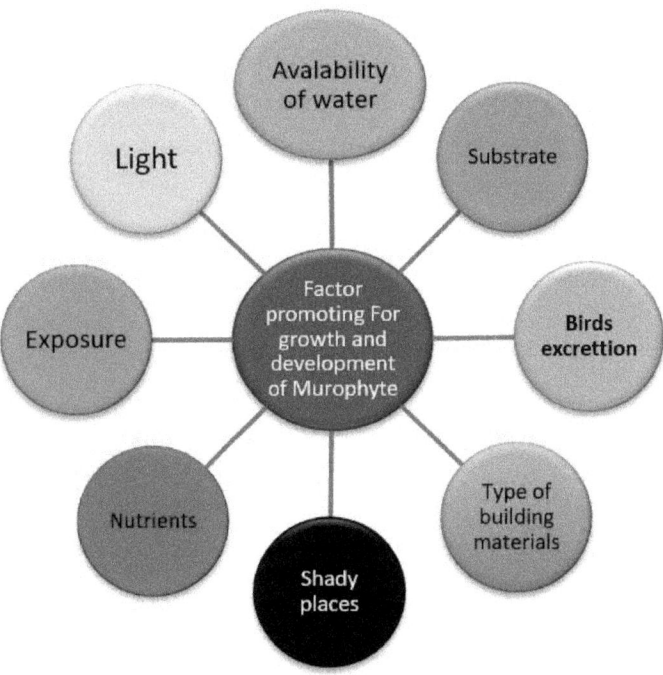

Figure 4.6: The most predominating factors responsible for growth and development of murophytes.

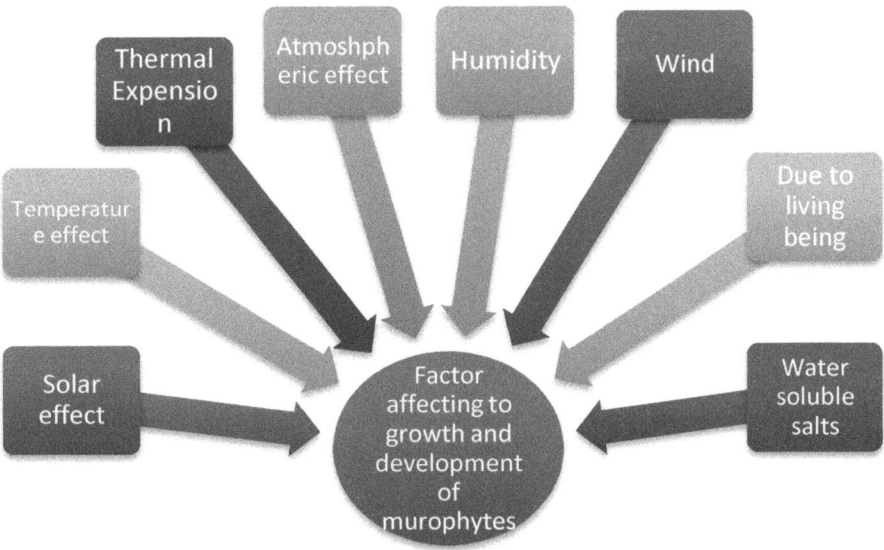

Figure 4.7: Some other factors for germination and growth of murophytes

Water

Water is an impartment factor to growth and development of murophyte (Figure: 4.8 (a and b). Naturally the availability of water varies with the type of surface and its exposure. It is one of the essential conditions for the establishment and maintenance of vegetation.

Figure 4.7: (a & b): Improper water management on roofExposure

The exposure of the wall is important above all, in relation to the main direction of the rain (Figure: 4.9 & 4.10). Arid wall exposed to the sun for many hours of the day determine strict selection of the murophytes. Southern exposures absorb more solar radiation than northern exposures. In mountain communities, northern exposures will have shorter growing seasons. In mountain communities gardeners often place warm season plants, like tomatoes, on the south side of buildings to capture more heat.

Figure 4.9: Heerapuri Colony, DDU Gorakhpur University campus, Gorakhpur.

Figure 4.10: Front wall of Botany Department, DDU Gorakhpur University, Gorakhpur.

Light

Light is essential for photosynthesis, a process by which plants manufacture their food. Therefore the quality duration and intensity of light available to the plants is of most important in their growth on monuments or buildings. The growth of murophytes is limited in condition of low light (Figure: 4.11 (a & b)).

a　　　　　　　　　　　　　　　　　　　**b**

Figure 4.11(a &b): The quality duration and intensity of light

Substrate

This is one of the key factors for evaluating the adaptability of plant is certain situations. The formation of substrate does not regard only the manner in which the wall is built but also biotic (decomposition by microorganism) and abiotic (climatic agents and atmospheric pollution) factors (Dwivedi & Anand, 2013). These factors contribute to the crumbling of lime mortor, leading to the formation of fissures and cavities within the walls. Substrate rich in detritus can form in these spaces with the auxiliary of atmospheric dust, bird excrement, human wastes, bryophytes, lichens, bacteria and fungi normally present in soil. Moss often creates the environment necessary for the germination of seeds in some cases the relations between tracheophytes and bryophytes are regulated by inhibitory allelophathic mechanisms. In fact substances which inhibit seed germination and root growth of higher plant have been isolated bryophytes. e.g., Lunaric acid from *Lunularia cruciata*(L).In other cases the moss gametophyte constituting on absorbent surface, collects dust and other material. The resulting substrate of organic and inorganic residues can host the germination of seeds. Plants surviving in such environments often have reduced vegetative and reproductive parts; since the mural habitat does not permit them to develop to normal size. Places facilitating the rooting of plants of this type may be protruding shelves or irregular surfaces which provide space for the build-up detritus or soil (Dwivedi & Anand 2013, 2014). The amount of substrate needed for Seed germination varies from species to species. Shrub and tree (chamaephytes, phanerophytes) require more substrate and therefore prefer to grow along earth- fill walls offering a substantial amount of soil.

Figure: 4.12 (a,b,c & d). Different types of substrate needed For seed germination varies from species to species.

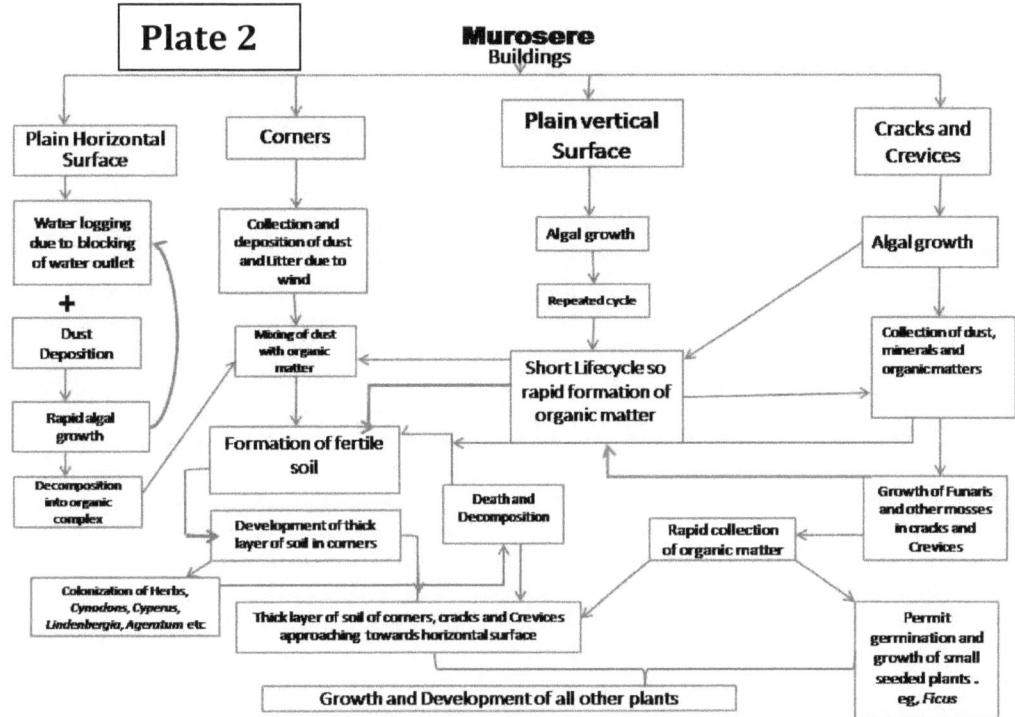

Nutrients

The availability and type of nutrients present in the substrate also play an important role in the growth of plant (Figure: 4.13(a &b)). Nutrients can be either organic or inorganic in nature. The organic nutrients may be either an impurity in the substrate or decomposition product of other organism. The inorganic nutrients are usually the mineral constituents of the substrates (Table: 4.4).

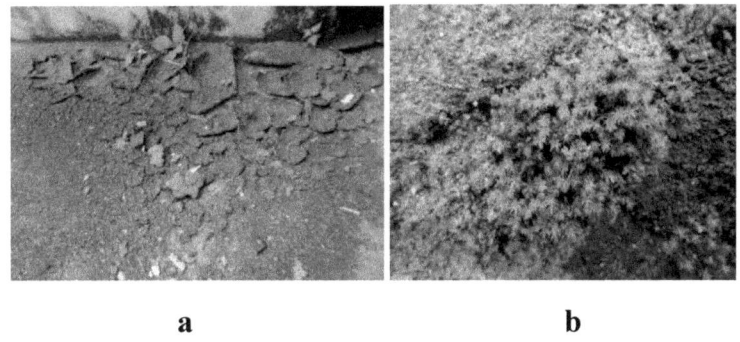

Figure 4.13(a&b): Dry biomass of lower plants

Essential Plant Nutrients			
Mineral	Non-Mineral		
	Macronutrients		Micronutrients
	Primary	Secondary	
Hydrogen	Nitrogen	Calcium	Boron
Oxygen	Phosphorus	Magnesium	Copper
Carbon	Potassium	Sulfur	Iron
			Chloride
			Manganese
			Molybdenum
			Zinc

Figure 4.4: Essential Plants Nutrients

One of the important facts for the murophytes is that, such plants produce tiny seeds. Birds and small animals such as bats, squirrel play very important role is dispersal and establishment of the plants over the buildings.

Bird's excretement

Their role in dispersal of seeds was confirmed through scatological studied. Birds and animals use trees for shelter, nesting, feeding, wintering, roosting etc., they enjoy eating plants fruits (Figure: 4.14) and consequently disperse seeds through their scat and droppings. Many animals dispose off their dropping on walls of the buildings (Figure: 4.15). The rain washes the droppings and the seeds are further dispersed. The plants seed are light in weight, hence easily shifted by flow of runoff and reach the appropriate germination sites.

Figure 4.14: Squirrel feeding on fruit of *Ficus benghalensis*.

Figure 4.15: Plants seed in bat (*Pteropus gianteus*) excreta.

Building Structure

The architecture of old buildings and the magnificent carvings for beautification provides more anchoring points for the settlement of seeds. Horizontal and vertical folds and joints in the carvings act as a capillary and facilitate the seed to settle with the movement of water (Lisci & Pacini, 1993). The uprooted or damaged plasters of a wall also provide favorable sites for germination of murophytes (Figure: 4.16 (a,b,c,d,e&f). Walls have many primary seed traps, where the seeds are initially captured in building. After the growth of the plants, walls are further damaged and they provide secondary and tertiary seeds traps too. This result in the successive damage of buildings and make them more vulnerable.

Figure 4.16(a, b, c, d, e & f):-The types of buildings like, old buildings uprooted or damaged plaster buildings, brick wall buildings, tiles protected buildings etc., of a wall and provides favorable sites for growth and germination of murophytes.

d : Experiments for Management of murophytes

Billion of currency is wasted each year just in the civil work of repair and maintenances of building; still the ancient building and monument are being destroyed continuously. The problem of plants growth over the monuments, if ignored in the initial stages, could prove quit costly both in terms of cost and manpower involved at later stages. Therefore, the trees, climbers and creepers growing over the structures should be removed as quickly and completely as possible. The mechanism of deterioration of stone of monuments by higher plant is quite complex. The biophysical decay is mainly due to growth and radial thickening of the roots of plant inside the stones which result in an increasing pressure on surrounding areas of the masonry. Compared to herbaceous plants, woody species specifically tree can cause much more damage due to extensive root system which can grow for meters in length, width and depth.

During study, *Ficus* species *F. religiosa, F. benghalensis, F. glomerata and F.virens* are found mainly responsible for biophysical weathering and are very much frequent in occurrence on historical ancient buildings in comparison to recently constructed buildings (Singh, 2010). Due to religious beliefs people avoid cutting or damaging *Ficus* plants. Some practices are adopted by local people, such as cutting of branches and stem, application of acid after cutting stem etc. to get rid of ruderal *Ficus* species and protect buildings; but these are not the permanent solutions and still building suffer. Looking to the type and extent of damage to these building, following measures are suggested for the protection and conservation of ancient heritage (Sitaraman *et al.*,2009).In the past the eradication of plants was achieved mainly by pulling out or by cutting and killing of the plant part by making use of certain chemicals.

To suggest prophylactic and curative measures, which can be practiced by the society to protect buildings have been suggested by (Yasin, 2007 &Singh, 2010).

Many methods can be used to control mural vegetation but often a combined programmed of holistic approach (manual and chemical method) is required to solve the problem at root level (Lisci & Pacini 1993).

Herbicides can also be classified by their "*site of action*" or the specific biochemical site that is affected by the herbicide. The site of action is a more precise description of the herbicide's activity. However, the terms "site of action" and *"mode of action"* are often used interchangeably to describe different groups of herbicides, as suggested by Amstrong; PSC 2778.

All the methods suggested for eradication of the murophytes can broadly be classified in to two categories:

1. **Physical methods**
   a. **Hand pulling**
   b. **Hand hoeing**
   c. **Mowing**
2. **Chemical methods**
   a. **Spray**
   b. **Drill and injection in the concrete**
   c. **Injection in the plants**

1. The Physical method of murophyts control

In this method the morophytes are controlled by uprooting them at their initial stages of developments (Figure: 4.17). The fully grown plants can be controlled using suitable sharp cutting instruments like khukuri, sickle etc. This method is not a permanent solution for the control of plant growth in the monument and historic buildings because plants like *Ficus religiosa* may grow with more vigour when they are cut owing to the phenomenon of apical dominance. However it may be very effective method for the prevention of plant growth when applied during initial stages of development (Yadav, 2009 & Mishra, 1995).

Physical method can further be classified as:

a. **Hand pulling**
b. **Hand hoeing**
c. **Mowing**
a. **Hand pulling**

The removal of murophyte by means of hand pulling also known as hand weeding is a very common and effective method of weed control as it removes every blade of murophyte.

Figure 4.17: Root of higher plants (Murophyte) absorbing nutrients from the organic complex of wall

The method is particularly suitable for the removal of annual plant, from those buildings where the growth is rather scanty. The method also eliminates the possibility of leaving behind unwanted chemicals which may affect the surface of the buildings. Besides being a very slow and tiresome process, the method involves some risk in the form of damage to adjoining surface if the growths are pulled out injudiciously. In order to eradicate perennial plants, the operation must be repeated from time to time.

b. Hand hoeing-

In this method tools and instruments like hand blade, sickles picks axes and spades are used for the removal of annual herbaceous plants (Figure: 4.18). The method involves the complete destruction of the top growth by cutting just below the crown of the plants. However repeated operations are necessary to achieve complete eradication of perennial growth as these are liable to regrow at the end of one season.

Figure 4.18: Hand hoeing

c. Mowing repeated cutting and defoliation:

This method may be extremely useful for the removal of perennial and woody plants as it not only prevents seed formation but also starves the subsurface parts. Repeated cutting is required to control the plant growth completely by this method and at no time is the plant permitted to replenish its food supply stored in the roots. However when the apical bud is cut off the lateral bud start developing into shoots. Therefore, as a consequence of the cutting operation, the stem may appear to be thickened initially rather than thinning. However, if cutting is continued persistently so as to keep the root reserves low, the stem will finally start thinning with a depleted food supply. Under such conditions the increase in the number of shoots may actually speed up the reduction of root reserves which will ultimately result in the death of the plant.

3. Chemical methods:

Since most of the manual or mechanical methods are labour intensive, the use of certain chemicals commonly known as herbicides has gained ground over the years. They have been one of the miracles to releasing thousand people from the drudgery of hand weeding. The herbicides are those chemical which are used to kill or retard the growth of an unwanted plant or weed (Figure: 4.19). The herbicides can be classified in several way based on their effect, translocation or mode of attack or action. A list of effective chemicals is given in the (Table 4.5).

Table 4.5: Herbicides also available in market:

No.	Common Name	Chemical name	Recommended dose	Type of plant to be controlled
1.	Atrazine	1-Chloro-3-ethylamino-5-isopropylamino-2,4,6-triazine	1-5 ml	Herbaceous weed
2.	2,4-D	2,4- Dichlorophenoxy acetic acid	1-ml or 0.5-1%	Herbaceous
3.	Paraquat, Gramoxone	1.1'-Dimethyl-4, 4'-bipyridinium ion (available as dichloride and di methyl sulphate.	0.1 -0.2 %	Herbaceous weed
4.	Glyphosate	N-(phophono- methyl) glycine	1-3 %	Herbaceous
5.	Dalapon	2,2-Diachloro propionic acid	1-5 %	Perennial weeds
6.	Picloram	4-Amino-3,5,6-trichloro picolinic acid(potassium salt)	0.5-1%	Broad leaf Perennial weeds

In physical method, tries to remove the plant completely from the monuments. If the plants are not possible to remove completely then use the chemical method.

The chemical can be used in 3 ways:

a. Spray

b. Drill and injection in the concrete

c. Injection in the plants

a. Spray

In this case herbicide like Glyphosate (Gramaxone) is sprayed over the plant trunk and after one to five days the photosynthesis process is arrested and the plant become black; also the green leaves change into black colour (Figure: 4.21).

b. Drill and injection in the concrete

In second case plant body cut down to root portion as for as possible, make hole using drilling machine. Then inject 1-3% aqueous sodium arsenate solution or latter should be preferred because of toxicity to human being and other animals for the first one. After three or four application of these chemicals, plants cut off surface are sealed by some sealing agent wax or cement and concrete (Figure: 4.20).

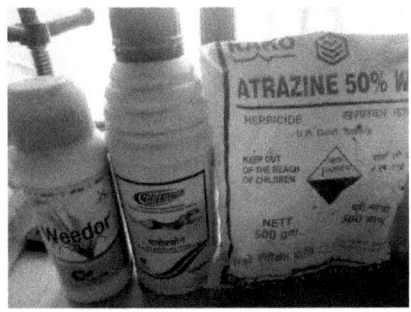 

Figure 4.19: Used herbicide. **Figure 4.20:** Treated plant with herbicide

c. Injection in the plants

In this method the herbicides are injected directly into the tree trunk or stem by a medical syringe (Mishra, 1995; Singh, 2010 & Yadav, 2009).

Usually one injection per (1-2 cm) thickness of plant is sufficient. The injection method is also suitable for bushes of more in diameter. The success of the treatment is however more dependent upon the type of the herbicide used and its concentration. Method like injection seems to be more useful as compared to foliar spray (Table 4.6).

Spray of Gramaxone in the beginning and after a few weeks, injection of 1% solution of sodium arsenate or 2.4 D is very effective in eradicating plants from the building and monuments (Figure: 20). These chemicals are very toxic and hence only trained persons should handle. While handling these chemical, protective gears like mask gloves spectacles and apron should be used. Accessories like spray pump; drilling machine, syringes etc. would be required during operation. After the plant is dead, it should be carefully removed by dismantling certain portions of the monuments. After removal of plant the cracks and gaps should also be repaired of the dismantled portion so as to prohibit further growth of plants (Yadav, 2009).

Monitoring of the treatment of the in (Figure: 4.22) was done even after 150 days, when it was recorded that the plant was completely dead. No further growth/germination /budding/sprouting of the plant was recorded even after 150 days.

Plates (Figure: 4. 23) show the impact of injection of saturated solution of NaCl at different time interval in *Ficus benghalensis* the most prominent murophyte. On Twenty fourth days the plant was recorded to be completely dead.

Sample (A)	Conc^n (ml)	Ficus benghalensis Days				
		1	2	3	4	5
Atrazine	1	-	-	-	-	+
	2	-	-	-	+	
	3	-	-	+		
	4	-	+			
	5	+				

Sample (B)	Conc^n (ml)	Ficus benghalensis Days				
		1	2	3	4	5
2,4.D	1	-	-		+	
	2	-	-	+		
	3	+				
	4					
	5					

Sample (C)	Conc^n (ml)	Ficus benghalensis Days				
		1	2	3	4	5
Gramoxone	1	-	-	+		
	2	+				
	3					
	4					
	5					

Figure: Sample (C)

Table 4.6 (a,b &c): Effect on *Ficus benghalensis* after injected with Atrazin, 2,4 D and Gramoxone with different volume and days.

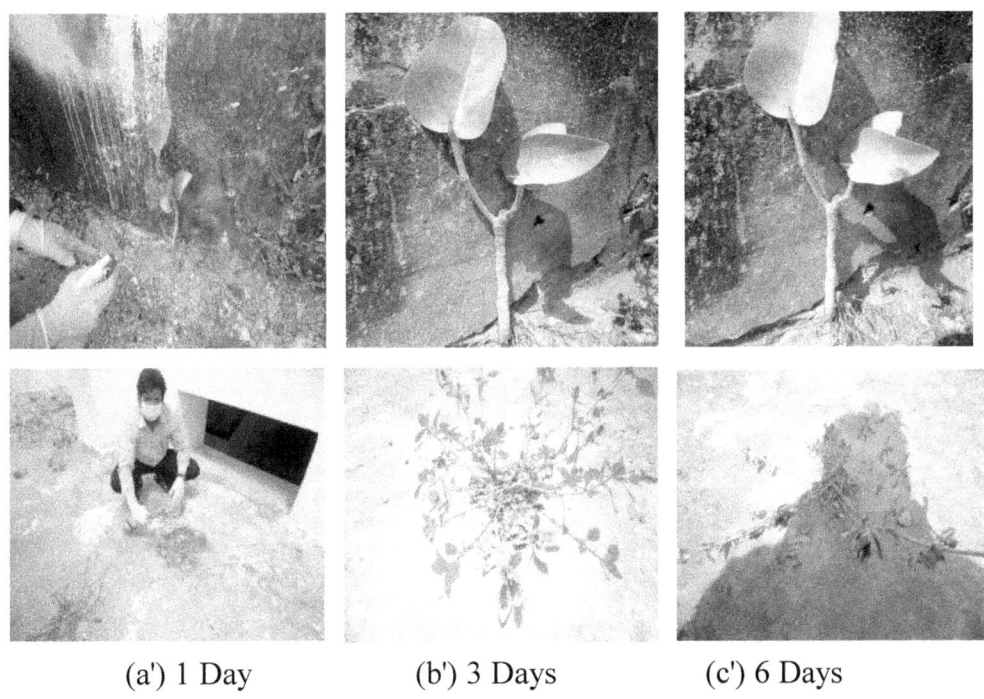

(a') 1 Day   (b') 3 Days   (c') 6 Days

Figure 4.21: Plates showing different stages of impact of Atrazin spray over the plants

Figure 4.22: Plates showing different stages of impact of 2,4 D injection in *Ficus benghalensis*.

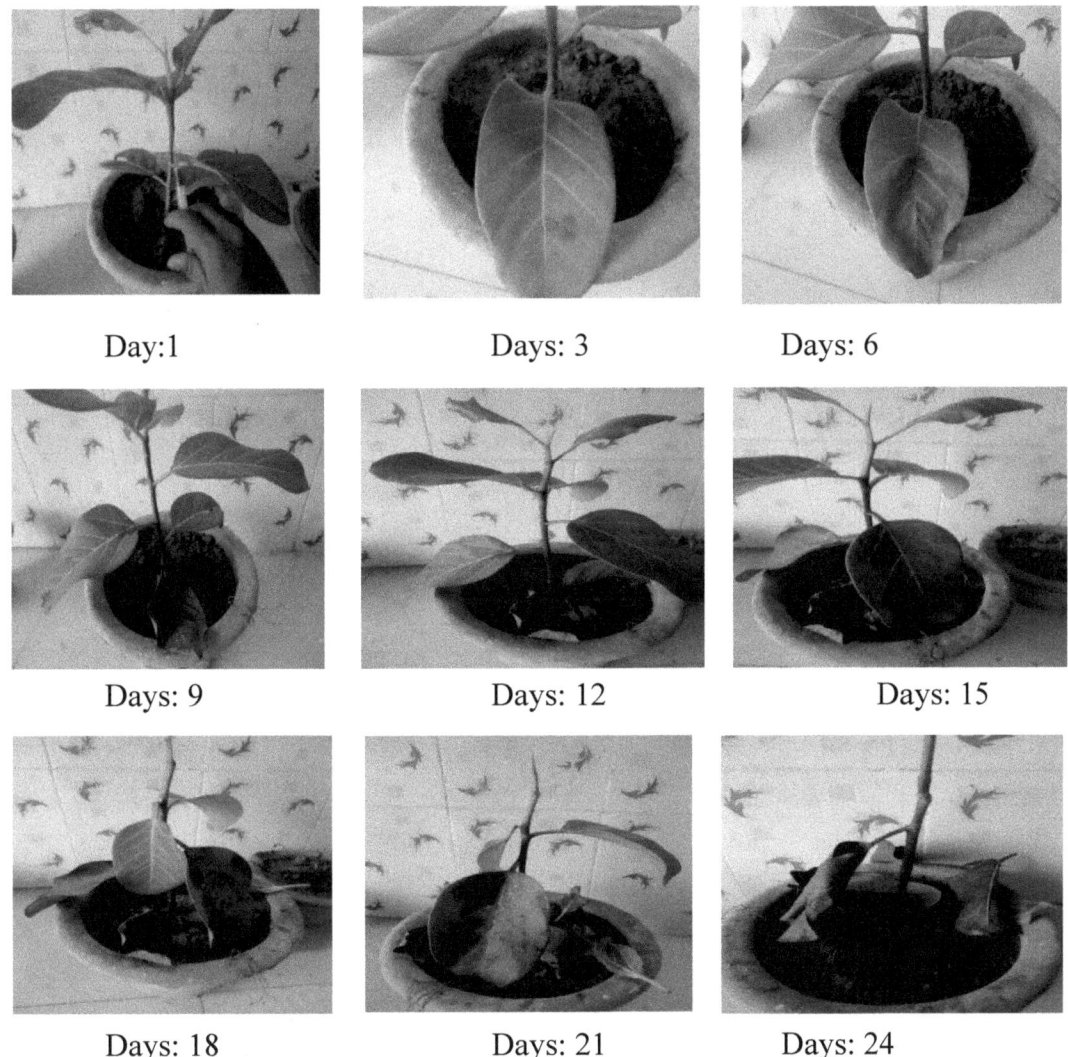

Figure 4.23: Plants showing the impact of injection of saturated solution of NaCl.

Plate: 1 Types of Buildings structure

A. *Concrete wall*
B. *Red stone*
C. *Mud wall*
D. *Tiles/Ceramics wall*
E. *Brick cement wall*
F. *Marble wall*

PLATE- 1

Plate 2: Murophytic species of different localities of Gorakhpur District

A. *Catharantus roseus*

B. *Ficus benghalensis*

C. *Ficus religiosa*
D. *Ficus glomerata*
E. *Lindenbergia sps.*
F. *Peperomia pellucida*
G. *Mosses*
H. *Mosses and Lindenbergia sps.*
I. *Adiantum sps.*
J. *Dryopteris bissetiana*

PLATE- 2

Plate 3: Murophyte on different localities

- **A.** *Plane Horizontal surface*
- **B.** *Plain Vertical surface*
- **C.** *Building roof/Ceiling*
- **D.** *Building terrace*
- **E.** *100 years old building*
- **F.** *Top of the wall*
- **G.** *Corner of wall*
- **H.** *From terrace to ground*

PLATE- 3

Plate 4: New reports of Murophytes From Gorakhpur

A. *Bombax ceiba*
B. *Trema orientalis*
C. *Catharanthus roseus*
D. *Cannabis sativa*
E. *Ricinus communis*
F. *Tridax procumbens*
G. *Tinospora cordifolia*
H. *Achyranthes aspera*

PLATE- 4

Chapter 5
Bibliographic Appraisal

Abllah, N. B. 2010. The assessment of building defects maintenance in hospital building. A thesis faculty of civil engineering and earth resources University Malaysia Pahang. 1-24.

Almeida, M. T; Mouga, T & Barracosa, P. 1994. The weathering ablity of higher plants. The case of Ailanthus altissima (Miller) Swingle. *International Biodeterioration and Biodegradation.* **33(4):** 333-343.

Altay, V; Ibrahim, I. Ozyigit & C. Yarci. 2010. Urban ecological characteristics and vascular wall flora on the Anatolian side of Istanbul, turkey, *Maejo. Int. J. Technol.* **4(3):** 483- 495.

Ashurst, J. & Ashurst, N. 1988. Practical building conservation, **vol. 1.** *Gower Technical press, Hants.* UK, pp. 20-26.

Bagdad, B; Taleb, A; Carlo I. I; Hadi, E. I & Dalimi, M. 2014. The vascular vegetation populating the flora in Building materials of Historic Monuments cities of the west central region of Morocco. *Open journal of Ecology.* **4:** 565-570.

Bhargav, J. S. 2012. Chemical weathering of archaeological monuments and their conservation, *Jour. Geol. Soc. India.* **80:** 148.

Boratynski, *et al.,* 2003. Ficus and Vegetation of walls in the town of Krosno Odrzanskie (Poland). *Collect. Bot. (Barcelona).* **26:** 129-139.

Brandes, D. 2002. Some remark on the flora of wall and ruins in eastern crete. *htt://opus.tubs.de/opus/Volltexte.* **30(6):** 291.

Caneva, G & Roccardi, A. 1991. Harmful flora in the conservation of Roman monuments. *In. Int. Congr. Biodet. Cultural Property, Lucknow.* 212- 218.

Caneva, G. and Salvadori, O. 1989. Biodeterioration of stone. In: L. Lazzarini and R. Pieper (Eds.), *Studies and Documents on the Cultural Heritage, No. 16. UNESCO, Paris,* pp. 182-234.

Cerejo, S; S. Rajdeo; M. Kalpit, & S. Rajendra. 2010. Chasmophytic flora of Bassein fort (Thane District), Maharashtra, India.*www.researchgate.net.* **1:** 54-58.

Dixit, S. N. 1983. Wall flora of Gorakhpur India. *Tropical Ecology.* 188-193.

Dos, R; Lombardi, V. A; J. A & R. A. De Figueiredo. 2006. Diversity of vascular plants growing on walls of a Brazilian city. *Urban Ecosyst.* **9:** 39-43.

Duchoslav, M .2002. Flora and vegetation of stony walls in East Bohemia (Czech Republic). *Pres. Pra.* **74:** 1-25.

Dwivedi, A. K & Anand, D. K. 2013. The Murophyte, *Indian Science Cruiser.* **27(1):** 32-35.

Dwivedi, A. K and Anand, D. K. 2014. Investigation of diversity in Murophytes in the campue of University in Gorakhpur, India. *IJPAES.* **4(3):** 569-575.

Dwivedi, A. K and Anand, D. K. 2014. Ficus is the most dominant murophyte. *J. Env. Bio. Sci.* **28(1):** 9-12.

Honeyborn, D. B. 1990. Weathering and decay of masonry. In *J. Ashurst and F. G. Dimes (Eds) Conservation of building and decorative stone*. Vol 1. Butterworth, Guildford, UK. Pp. 153-184.

Hussian, S. S; Ahmad, M; Siddiqui, M. F; Khan, N & Rao, T. A. 2011. Ediphytes of Karachi. *FUUAST. J. BIOL.* **1(2):** pp. 87-91.

Garg, K.L; Kamal, K. J & Mishra, A. K. 1995. Role of fungi in the deterioration of wall painting. *Science of the total Environment.* **167**. 225-271.

Khan, D .2011. Nicotiana Plunbaginifolia VIV. An Addendum to the Ediphytes of Karachi. *Fuuast J. Biol.* **1(2):** 93-94.

Kolbek, J and Volachovic, M. 1996. Plant communities on walls in North Korea. *A preliminary report Thaiszia J. Bot. Kosice.* **6:** pp. 67-75.

Kumar, R & Sharma, Y. K. 2014. Identification of vascular floristic composition growing on building: A slow poison for building life. *J. Biol. Chem. Research.* **31(1):** 380-398.

Kumar, R & A. V. Kumar. 1999. Biodeterioration of stone in tropical environments: an overview / *The Getty Conservation Institute*. 1- 75.

Lanikova, D & Iososova, Z. 2009. Rocks and walls: Natural Versus Secondary habitats. *Folia Geobot.* **44:** 263- 280.

Lawson, M & Callaghan. D. 1995. A critical analysis of the role of trees in damage to low rise buildings. *J. Arboricuture.* **21 (2):** 90-97.

Lesser, L. M. 2001. Hardscape damage by tress roots, *Journal of Arboriculture.* **27(5):** 272-276.

Lisci, M and Pacini, E. 1993. Plant growing on the walls of Italion Town 1. Sites and distribution. *Phyton Horn, Australia.* **33(1):** 15-26.

Lisci, M and Pacini, E. 1993. Plant growing on the walls of Italian Town 2. Reproductive Ecology, *Giornale botanico Iitaliano.* **127(6):** 1053-1078.

Li H, Qian S, Li Ting, Jim C.Y, Jin C, Zhao Li, Lin D, S K, & Yang Y. 2019. Masonry walls as sieve of urban plant assemblages and refugia of native species in Chongqing, China. *ELSEVIER, Landscape and Urban Planning.* **191:** 103620.

Mishre, A. K, Kamal K. J & Garg, K. l. 1995. Role of higher plants in the deterioration of historic buildings. *Science of the Total Environmental.* **167 (1-3):** 375-392.

Motti, R & Stinca. A. 2011. Analysis of the biodeteriogenic vascular flora at the Royal palace of Portici in Southern Italy, *International Biodeterioration and Biodegradation.* **65:** 1256- 1265.

Nedelcheva, A. 2011. Observations on the wall flora of Kyustendil (Bulgaria). *Euras. J. Biosc.* **5:** 80-90.

Nedelcheva. A & Vasileva, A. 2009. Vascular plants from the old walls in Kystendil (Southwestern Bulgaria), *Biotechnal and Biotechnal*, EQ,23/SF special Edition/online. **9:** 154-157.

Nimis, P. L. 2001. Artistic and historical monuments: *Threatened Ecosystems Man and the Environments.* **2(4):** 557-570.

Pandey, S. Kumar Neetesh & Singh, S, K. 2016. Potentiality of wall flora in characterization of urban ecology, *IJARIIE,* **2(6):** 1683-1688.

Pavlova, D Tonkov, S. 2005. The wall flora of the Nebet Tepe Architectural Reserve in the city of Plovdiv (Bulgaria), *Acta Bot. Croat.* **64 (2):** 357–368.

Payne, R. M. 1978. The flora of walls in South-eastern Essex. *Watsoni.* **12:** 41-46.

Pocock, C. 2008. An investigation into plant species composition on the Roman wall in Silchester, Hampshire, UK. *Geoverse.* 1-18.

Presland, J. 2008a. Dry stone wall in winsley. Wiltshire, *Botany.* **10:** 23-28.

Presland, J. 2008b. The flora of wall: drystone verses mortared. *BSBI News.* **108:** 7-11.

Presland, J. 2008c. it's there a limestone drystone wall community? *BSBI News.* **109:** 9-12.

Reddy N. C. M. 2012. Ficus the survival specialists in flowering plants world. http://www.thehindu.com/life and style/homes and gardens/article 3456265.

Rajalakshmi, S and Shanthi, Dr. K. 2012. Survey of wall flora in Gingee fort and uncared gopuras in Gingee taluk, villupuram district. *International journal of ayurvedic & herbal medicine.* **2(5):** 810-816.

Saeed, M; Khan, Z. Ud Din & Ajaib, M. 2012. Some phytosociological studies of chasmophytes and Ediphytes of Lahore city, *Pak. J. Bot.* **44:** pp. 165-169.

Satriani, A; Ajaib, A; Proto, M; & Bavusi, M. 2010. Building damage caused by tree roots: Laboratory experiments of GPR and ERT surveys, *Adv. Geosci.* **24:** 133-137.

Segal, S. 1969. Ecological notes on wall vegetation, *Dr. W. Junk Publication.* The Hague. Pp. 325.

Shah, R. P and Shah, N. R .1992. Growth of plants on monuments, *conservation Information Network (BCIN).* **26:** 29-34.

Sharma, K & Lanjewar, S. 2010. Biodeterioration of ancient Monument (Devarbija) of Chhattisgarh by Fungi. *Journal of Physiology.* **2(11):** 47-49.

Singh, H; Verma, A; Kumar, R; Joshi, B and Meena, D. 2011. Diversity of woody and non woody forestry species in Budaun district of uttar Pradesh. India, *Researcher.* **3(12):** 1-7.

Singh, M and Kumar, M. 2013. Study of plant diversity of Jind district, Harayana, India. *Asian Journal of plant sciences and Research.* **3(3):** 44-53.

Singh, S; Katewa, S. S and Sharma, S. K. 2010. Study on various species of Ficus Genus growing as Ruderal flora on buildings Southern Rjesthan. *The Ecoscan.* **4(1):** 97-102.

Singh, A. 2011. Observations on vascular wall flora of Banaras Hindu University Campus, India. *Bullet. Environ, Pharmacol. & Life Sci.* **1(1):** 33-39.

Singh, D. K & Singh, R. 2014. Study of Angiospermic wall floristic composition of city buxar (Bihar), India. *Journal of Pharmacognosy and Phytochemistry*. **2(5)**: 52-54.

Sitaramam, *et al.,* 2010. Ficus religiosa, habit, habitat and religious. *Current Science.* **98(7):** 885.

Sitaramam, V; Jog. S. R and Tetali, P. 2009. Ecology of Ficus religiosa accounts for its association with religion. *Current Science,* vol. **97**: 5-10.

Sitaramam, V; Jog, S. R. and Tetali, P. 2009. Ecology of Ficus religiosa accounts for its association with religion. *Current Science.* **97(5)**: 637-640.

Syed, S. H; Ahmed, M; Siddiqui, M; Khan, N & Toqeer, A. R. 2011. Ediphytes of Karachi, *Fuuast. J. Biol.* **1(2): 87-97.**

Tiano, P. 2002. Biodegradation of cultural heritage; decay mechanisms and control methods, *CNR - Centro di studio sulle "Cause Deperimento e Metodi Conservazione Opere d'Arte", Via G. Capponi 9, 50121 Firenze, Italy.* pp. 1-37.

Varshney, C. K. 1971. Observations on the Varanasi wall flora. *Vegetatio.* **22(6):** 355-372.

Williams, L. 1986. Observation on the flora of wall habitats on yell, Shetland. Ecological studies in the maritime approaches to the Shetland oil terminal, *Report of the polytechnic Expedition to Shetland School of life sciences.* 1-6.

Woodell, S. 1979. The flora of walls and pavings. In Laurie I. C. (ed.) Nature in cities, *John Wiley & Sons.* Chichester. Pp. 135-157.

Winkler, E. M. 1975. Stone decay by plants and animals In: stone Properties, Durability's in Man's Environments. *Springer.* New York. 154-164.

Yadav, O. P. 2009. Eradication of plants and trees from historic building and monuments, *ancient_Nepal_144_03 pdf. 1-5.*

Yaldiz, E. 2010. Climatic effect on monumental building orchid Republic of Macedonia engineering faculty of architecture department architecture, Turkey. 1-10.

Yasin, M. F. M; Zaidi, M. A. & Hamid, Y. 2007. The unwanted plants and its effect to the building in Malaysian hot and humid climate. *Australian Institute of building surveyors (ABIS).* Pp. 307-320.

www.ingramcontent.com/pod-product-compliance
Lightning Source LLC
LaVergne TN
LVHW070527070526
838199LV00073B/6715